coaching
IS FOR EVERYONE

Learn How to be

Your Own C

at Any Ag

TERRI LEVINE
Master Certified Coach

New York

Coaching is for Everyone

By Terri Levine
© 2008 All rights reserved.

ISBN: 978-1-60037-396-1 (Paperback)
ISBN: 978-1-60037-397-8 (Hardcover)

LCCN: 2008920325

Published by:

MORGAN · JAMES
THE ENTREPRENEURIAL PUBLISHER
www.morganjamespublishing.com

Morgan James Publishing, LLC
1225 Franklin Ave. Suite 325
Garden City, NY 11530-1693
800.485.4943
www.MorganJamesPublishing.com

Cover & Interior Designs by:

Megan Johnson
Johnson2Design
www.Johnson2Design.com
megan@Johnson2Design.com

Habitat
for Humanity®
Peninsula
Building Partner

A Word from the Author

I have so many people to thank for this book now being in your hands. First of all, my Creator who inspired me to share with you. Next, a little girl from grade school…

Many years ago when I lived in Yonkers, New York, and was in elementary school, I met a girl named Jackie. Jackie came to school by bus and was living in an orphanage. As I got to understand through Jackie what this meant, I felt sad. My family didn't have a lot of money, but I had parents, an apartment, and the security of knowing I had a home.

The day before Halloween I was talking to Jackie on the playground about trick or treating and she said she didn't get to do that. I decided right then that I would get as much candy as I could for Jackie.

We lived in a cooperative where there were six apartments per unit and the number of units we had was hard to count! I first went unit to unit and had to go home because I couldn't carry the amount of candy I had. Thinking back, there must have been at least five dozen units in the coop.

That Halloween night I left again, this time armed with two giant shopping bags. I tackled individual homes in the neighborhood, and then I realized there were two tall buildings called condos—they looked like apartments to me. Anyway, I had a friend who lived in one. I rang her doorbell and she was home and then she helped me do both tall buildings.

It was late and dark and I had to get home.

My mother thought I collected the candy for myself (I never liked candy!) and she wondered why I needed so much. When I explained to her about Jackie, she helped me package all the candy up nicely.

My sister came home and brought me a giant plastic pumpkin filled with candy and a tall object with a skeleton head on the top, also filled with candy. I told her thanks and told her that this year Jackie was getting it all.

My mom had to help me to school and we walked carrying all these bags and the pumpkin and skeleton head. Then, I waited outside for the bus, and as soon as I saw Jackie I pulled her into our classroom and gave her the bags. She cried and cried. I've never forgotten this experience and the love and compassion I felt for her. I wanted to do more.

Ever since Jackie, which I think was in the third or fourth grade, I have lived my life on a mission to serve others and help others. When I make money, it *feels* good to me because I am then able to help others who are in need.

My vision is to give away 90% of what I earn and live on 10%.

Sure I could have another car, a newer car, a bigger home, a vacation home...who knows what else? But I want to give more, and so I enjoy my life with what I have and find causes I believe in. I take great joy in sharing my wealth with others.

This, in fact, is what drives me to make money.

Jackie, wherever you are, I am most grateful to you. You touched my heart and soul and I'll never forget the beauty you brought to my life.

I hope I can continue to pay it forward in bigger and bigger ways.

My thanks also goes to Mark Victor Hansen for fully supporting me and being excited about this book and believing the world needs to have this book in their hands. And to David L. Hancock at Morgan James who knew instantly this book had to be. With my deepest respect and appreciation to you all,

"T"

My Goal Is YOUR Success!

Terri Levine, The Guru of Coaching SM
http://www.CoachInstitute.com

Table of Contents

Coaching is for Everyone

Foreword

Oh! The places you'll go!

– Dr. Seuss

Y es, coaching is the new mantra! Coaching paves the way to an exciting world of opportunities, and in this ever-increasing competitive scenario, coaching is a god sent gift! When I learned coaching skills, I knew that all the self-help seminars and books I had experienced were nothing compared to these hidden skills. I had gone to self-help seminars for years and read books galore and spent money on trying to improve myself starting with eight-track tapes to cassettes and finally CDs and DVDs. Until I discovered the principles of coaching 10 years ago, nothing impacted my life for a long period of time, nothing stuck, and nothing really got me where I wanted to be in my life, relationships, or my career. When I learned coaching skills I realized that I needed to live as a coach and to be a coach. In the process, I got to really know my authentic self. I have created more joy, fun, prosperity, and ease in my life, and my relationships with friends and family have deepened because of my coaching skills. I know it is cliché to say, "My life changed," but mine really did. From weight loss without dieting to an income larger than I could have ever dreamed of to owning the business of my dreams I can honestly say nothing in my life is the same. My relationships to close friends and community have deepened, my spirituality has heightened, and my ability to travel expanded my understanding of the world. I am a changed person.

Coaching is for Everyone

I was so deeply enthralled with these skills that I went on to leave my corporate job and become a life and business coach. Later I founded one of the world's renowned coach-training schools (www.CoachInstitute.com), teaching others to become coaches. I discovered that many people joined the school just because they wanted coaching skills and not necessarily to be a coach as their profession. People around the world recognize how profound these skills are and yearn for them.

Now, I am revealing to you basic self-coaching skills—skills you have probably never been taught—because I know you deserve to life the life you deeply desire. It will be up to you to take these skills on and practice them full out. You won't have the benefit of the human interaction my coach training students have, but I know that if you commit yourself to practicing these skills, you will succeed and the lessons you learn here will change your life.

Self-coaching is an interactive and ongoing way to create fulfilling results in your personal and professional life. Through the self-coaching process, you will deepen your experiences, improve your performance, and enhance your quality of life. Self-coaching can be said to reincarnate your life!

Self-coaching creates a platform where you meet yourself face-to-face and evaluate your attitudes about yourself, and therein lays your strength, the power to rise. As Socrates advised, **"Know thyself. Once you come face to face with yourself and what you really are, you can do something about your limitations."**

There's no such thing as a "born coach." Just like there's no such thing as a "born doctor" or a "born lawyer." Self-coaching skills are to be learned and imbibed like anything else. And the key to nurturing and honing your self-coaching skills lies in the folds of **Coaching Is For Everyone.**

Coaching Is For Everyone will surely prove to be a knowledge powerhouse that will teach you skills you have never learned before. The essence of this book is to provide you the inside scoop on how to skyrocket your life and career with a system of practical self-coaching steps that are easy to learn and fun to use. No theoretical mumbo jumbo or outdated 1940s' methodologies.

Coaching Is For Everyone will not only enlighten you about the finer aspects of self-coaching but usher in an environment that will save you countless hours of trial and error, allow you to focus on the things that really work, and build upon your existing skills and expertise. It will become your bible as you read it over and over. And each time you do, you will turn up another batch of gems that just keep honing your skills!

Within you is your mind, an intricate computer that stores the thoughts that you choose day by day. These are molds that program and shape your life. Wise sages of all times have realized this. Marcus Aurelius wrote, **"Look well into thyself. There is a source which will always spring up if thou wilt always search there."**

Thus your life is an extension of your thoughts; you can never escape yourself. That is the focus of this book—you and your inner resources. Regardless of your age, occupation or position in life, this book is intended for you.

Terri Levine, The Guru of Coaching SM

Coaching is for Everyone

Introduction

You can have anything you want if you want it enough. You must want it with an exuberance that erupts through the skin and joins the energy that created the world

– Sheila Graham

K nowledge is power, and in this quest for self-advancement, you are about to begin a new learning adventure that will not only change your skills but may well shift your life and the way you view yourself. I want this journey to be as easy as possible for you despite its significance. In order to assist you as you embark on a unique series of transitions, I want to give you a brief overview of some of the places you'll go and the commitments you will need to make as you travel. I will provide you with some maps you can use along the way.

I want to make it clear that although I am a professional coach and I teach coaching skills to people who want to be professional coaches, too, coaching skills are not the domain of professional coaches only. Self-coaching is meant for everyone, and over the last 10 years I have taught these skills to thousands of people throughout the world. People of different cultures, occupations, and ages have journeyed together through the experience and become more aware of the significance of self-coaching. The reason I wrote this book is to teach you self-coaching skills so you can have more of what you want in your life and attract it with great ease. All these chapters, the

Coaching is for Everyone

various sections, the technical and the not-so-technical facets may at first seem overwhelming. Indeed, this book is comprehensive, derived from my years of research and professional experience.

Here are some suggestions to help you make this journey smooth and effortless while getting the most possible value. First, I encourage you to go slow. This is weighty material. You will absorb it better and more easily if you are willing to be patient. I also remind you to be sure you read each chapter again and again, so if something doesn't "click" the first time, try it again. And make sure you read the chapter called "Tuning In"—alone! You will find it fascinating and compelling instead of difficult and demanding. I also want you to have fun. Yes! In spite of its comprehensive structure, this book makes for an interesting read. It opens the door to the life-changing and exciting world of self-coaching. There's no lecturing or nagging here. You are getting to know yourself and your own attributes, with retrospection and reflection that even extend to your relationships. A wise coach I know once said, **"If you're not having fun yourself, you're doing it wrong."** And I wholeheartedly agree. Keep balance and fun at the top of your list and you will create a great life for yourself.

My intention is that by the time you complete this book, you will be comfortable using self-coaching skills to spearhead your new life. You will also have been introduced to coaching. You'll understand why everyone needs coaching skills and that everyone has the potential to be a coach. I also want you to be clear that you must participate fully in this book. This is about you. You determine what commitments you are willing to make in order to develop your self-coaching skills.

Moreover, as you read this book, you will find that it is meant to be interactive. You can be a participant or a spectator, but isn't that the way life is? Well, this adventure is designed for you to experience and discuss a lot of chunks of your life so you can better answer the question, **"Who am I?"** So as you begin your quest, please keep paper and pen handy, because on the way, along with interesting facts, you will enjoy some thrilling practical play work too. Remember, thoughts will be lost forever unless captured by pen or purpose!

When I coach clients I give them what I refer to as "play work" after most sessions. I do this to reinforce what they need to learn and for them to trigger the self-coaching skills they need. I call it "play work" because it is work for you to do and at the same time I want you to bring lightness, a sense of humor and a sense of childlike learning, to each play-work adventure. Do each activity from your heart in a light and playful way rather than making it a difficult chore. So, you will find play work throughout our "coaching" here. Please realize this is paramount to your inhaling this self-coaching so you have these skills forever. I know that you may want to rush on to the next chapter and I request you pause and do the work. Enjoy and let the knowledge run deep into you!

PLAY WORK

- ✓ What three commitments are you willing to make to yourself to fully master self-coaching skills?
- ✓ What are three attributes or characteristics that you would like to use every day as a person who is using self-coaching skills?

Coaching is for Everyone

Philosophy of Self-Coaching

That action is best which procures the greatest happiness for the greatest numbers.

– Francis Hutcheson

Before I enrolled to study to become a coach I decided to hire my own coach. I had done so much work on myself over the years but always felt something was missing and something was off. I had no idea what this was, and from the outside I looked successful. I had a nice home, nice cars, went on great trips, had a loving husband, many wonderful friends, a high-paying, high-profile job...but I wasn't fulfilled. I actually remember feeling guilty about not being happy while having so much. I hired a coach because I wanted to find this missing link. Within a few months' time I realized the inner link for me was about not understanding what I really wanted from my life and not having skills to listen to my inner voice, which I call my inner coach. You know, that intuitive gut feeling you have, that inner sense, that voice that tries to speak to you. As I learned to be quiet and listen to that voice, I knew instantly that I was meant to be a coach. Within months I had quit my job, lost weight, made wonderful new friends, developed a community of love and support, and connected to my spiritual beliefs.

Then when I began training as a coach, I realized that before I could coach clients I needed to work even more deeply on myself, and just meeting with my coach every week wasn't growing me as much as I wanted to

Coaching is for Everyone

grow. I developed a process for growing myself using coaching skills, and I call this "self-coaching." This meant I was activating within myself the coaching skills I was learning, and I practiced them and over time was able to use them without thinking. It was almost like they got into my DNA.

I am here as your coach to teach you these self-coaching skills and to help you activate them within yourself. When you have these skills you will easily discover, clarify, and align yourself with what you want to achieve. You will find that you are tuned in to your authentic, beautiful inner self.

Self-coaching is built on the principle of honoring yourself as the expert in your personal and professional life and seeing yourself as creative, re-sourceful, and whole. Always remember, YOU are a magnificent jewel and are even more beautiful with all your imperfections!

When you breathe in this concept you can see how when you learn self-coaching skills you enhance your sense of self and value yourself so much more. You raise your self-esteem and self-confidence and love yourself from within. What you will also come to know is that through self-coaching skills you will also learn to appreciate and value other people and their worth.

You picked up this book because you want more in your life and you are ready to let in self-coaching skills to improve your life. I acknowledge you for this. When I learned coaching skills, I was amazed at what changed in my life, and I continue to be amazed at what shows up in the lives of my clients and my coaching students.

You will notice that things shift and change as you learn these skills. New patterns will emerge as you immerse yourself in this self-coaching pro-gram. You will discover things about yourself that you never knew, forgot, or were hidden to you. Instead of looking to others for ideas, you will begin to self-generate solutions and strategies. And I am certain you will hold yourself responsible and accountable, versus being a victim or a blamer.

As you learn self-coaching skills, you will find that you are more in tune with yourself. Knowing yourself more deeply means being in tune with your "personal core." You will resonate quickly and easily with who you really are in there and always hold your authentic person in high regard. Your authentic self is that little child you were before you were told "no" and "stop" and you "should" or "should not" by your parents, teachers, clergy members, friends, and society. This authentic self still lives deep within you, and when you get in touch with it your life will be more peaceful and effortless. When you know your authentic self it only takes a moment to make decisions because you can quickly tap into what you do or don't want. You also will have great clarity about what you are willing to have in your life and work and what you are willing to do or change to get what you want.

The best self-coaching always keeps your personal core at the forefront and honors your inner authentic self. Everything in your self-coaching holds at the forefront your values and strengths melded with what you want to allow in and to experience. As you do this type of self-coaching, you will see how easy it becomes to add strategies to help you achieve your goals, because for once you will really know what your goals are.

I find that when coaching students begin to learn this process they expect they will have no bumps in the road. In my experience the best learning does have the bumps. In fact it is not unusual to become "stuck" while using self-coaching skills. If you do, just always remember your personal core and hold yourself in high regard with plenty of self-love. Then take a moment and see what powerful observation to make of yourself or what powerful question to ask of yourself. These are skills you will learn shortly. When you have learned the self-coaching skills from this book you will quickly identify how to move along when you feel stuck. Getting unstuck will become one of your most powerful self-coaching tools.

I want you to know that I view you as my client and I am here as your coach. We will be in partnership and we are on this journey together. As you master basic self-coaching skills such as the importance of truth and directness, you will start to accept the interplay of these concepts in coaching yourself and later learn to use coaching skills in dealing with your relationships, too. The focus always starts by activating coaching skills in yourself. Later you can shift to using coaching skills with your parents, children, partners, friends, employer, employees, and others in your life.

Self-coaching has a specific orientation that is very different from teaching yourself something new. I am sure you have read many self-help books, gone to many self-help seminars and listened to self-help CDs. All of those things are based on teaching yourself something new. One of the major differences you will notice here is that when you self-coach you are not the leader and you don't preach or dictate to yourself. Instead you tune in to your inner thoughts and become a very good listener to your deep thoughts. You really get what you need and it goes right into your cellular memory. This is the polar opposite of teaching yourself something new and then not using it or forgetting it without a care. Through coaching yourself you can stand firmly for what you believe. Once you are aware of the differences between training yourself or teaching yourself and coaching yourself, you will begin to understand what attitudes and habits you must change and accept to self-coach.

As you go about the following play work, please don't take the questions lightly. They are not as simple as they seem. Good luck to you!

PLAY WORK

- ✓ What three attitudes must you change in order to maintain a more loving relationship with yourself?

- ✓ What are three ways you can appreciate yourself more?

SELF-COACHING IS NOT THERAPY

Unlike therapy, which focuses on the past, self-coaching focuses on the future. Self-coaching is not emotional healing; instead, it focuses on emotional strength. Self-coaching does not do what therapy does. Therapy focuses on the past's impact on today and resolution of the past in order to move into the present and forward. Self-coaching looks into the future, focusing on the past in order to clarify strengths and patterns. Self-coaching takes you forward, and it does not depend on resolving the past to do it. Self-coaching skills do not make you a mental health therapist who can deal with mental disorders. I caution you that self-coaching is not the answer for you if you are emotionally unstable or traumatized or have difficulty functioning effectively. Self-coaching enables you to become empowered and to be fully capable of expressing and handling your emotions, and because you are emotionally strong and ready, you are immediately capable of moving forward in your life.

One of my potential clients wasn't sure if she needed a therapist or a coach. I asked her if she was willing to take actions and move forward. I asked her if she had the ability to look at the future without constantly reflecting on the past. When she told me she was ready to "march on" and that she "didn't give a hoot" about the past, only then did this person became my coaching client. Another potential client showed up and during our first few minutes together she could not stop talking about her past experiences at all and could not relate to the present without tying in the past. I encouraged her to work with a therapist first and then later, when she could take forward actions, to call me and I'd be delighted to work with her then and only then.

SELF-COACHING KNOWS YOU ARE THE EXPERT FOR YOUR LIFE AND WORK

People often hire experts to assist them with their lives and work. Many times people hire consultants for technical, professional, or experiential expertise. In a consulting scenario, the consultant is expected to review and analyze situations, offer an opinion on the cause or problem behind the situation, and create a recommended solution for you.

However, when you instead decide to take charge of your own life, you no longer need consultants. With the self-coaching skills you are about to learn, you understand that you are the expert in your own life. A loving attitude about helping yourself is all that is needed. You can look inward for advice, opinions, or suggestions and no longer feel you need to rely on outside experts. Instead, you learn to cultivate a deep understanding of who you are. You have tools and techniques to create the space and structure to find your own answers and to know that the answers you generate are the right ones for you.

No one really knows you but you. The rest of us have ideas and thoughts and feelings about you, and we take what is right for us based on our lives and our beliefs and project that on you. When I wanted to quit my job my family didn't have my answer. My father thought that giving up my career, college education, and high-paying job was frankly very foolish. My husband, who was supportive and never said a word, feared that I would not make it in my own business. Several friends thought I was a bit nuts for giving up a successful job. I went inside myself, and only I could know what was right for me.

Once you know how to coach yourself, you can take your coaching skills and expand them to your relationships. You will see that having coaching skills makes you a better parent, boss, and person by knowing how to listen deeply and connect with others and to come from love when offering advice, opinions, or suggestions. Learning not to judge others and to fully accept them and allow them to be the unique gems they are will create relationships built of trust and love. You'll know coaching skills and yet won't feel compelled to give advice. You will know what kinds of questions to ask and observations to make of others and will not be attached to what they decide, because you will give them the space to make their own choices. You will share your observations and truths with them in such a way that it always supports people in making their own choices and remaining responsible for their own actions. Self-coaching enables you to form strong and healthy relationships with others based on knowing yourself better. With these coaching skills you will also have better relationships with others. You will know and respect limits and learn to maintain and give personal space.

SELF-COACHING IS SELF-LOVE

To understand self-coaching, you must know that the entire premise of self-coaching is about treating yourself with dignity. Once you fully love and accept yourself you can also then embrace others with dignity as free and equal human beings. Remember, all self-coaching starts with acceptance and self-love. I came to coaching thinking I had a lot of self-respect and self-confidence. As I worked with my coach and later as I developed the "self-coaching" process I am sharing with you here, I realized that I had many fears about myself and many doubts about my abilities and talents. I even believed somewhere down deep that I was "stupid." But I did not know this and could not heal and love myself until I allowed this story to surface. Then I learned specific self-coaching techniques to fully embrace myself and deeply connect to "me." I know how to honor myself and believe in myself and am filled with self-love. I am my own best friend and the champion for Terri Levine.

To embrace coaching skills and have them become part of "who" you are and how you think and feel it is important not to turn coaching on and off. Instead, conduct yourself in a manner that brings credit to you, others, and the process of self-coaching. Always use your best self-coaching skills and commit to enhance your understanding of self-coaching skills and continue your growth and learning. Self-coaching takes practice. I encourage you to freely share your coaching skills with others interested in learning coaching skills for the purpose of increasing mutual levels of knowledge and understanding. If you decide you want more advanced training, practice and assistance, www.CoachInstitute.com is your resource.

Since you are now more familiar with self-coaching, here is your play work. Happy sailing!

PLAY WORK

✓ What do you want to accomplish with self-coaching?

SELF-COACHING COMPETENCIES

Now let me discuss the core self-coaching competencies that will support greater understanding about the skills and approaches within the self-coaching arena. Each of these will be covered in more detail in the upcoming chapters. I introduce them to you now because they make up the philosophy behind coaching. These core skills will also assist you in identifying your current skills and measuring the skills you need to learn. I know you may feel tired already. If all of this seems "too much," please relax and be patient. Each of the competencies will be an old and familiar friend by the time you finish your journey. Don't forget that I am here with you as your coach!

Each of the core skills sits as an individual competency and is not weighted---each is given equal importance and considered a core skill for anyone practicing self-coaching. For now, just let them in and later you will learn how to become competent with each one. Simply let this information in.

HONORING YOURSELF

All self-coaching is based on the overarching competency of honoring yourself. This establishes the tenor and tone for actually using coaching skills to improve yourself. Mastery of self-coaching competencies creates a great coaching space where you are free to tell the truth to yourself, do your work, grow, move forward, and achieve your goals. As you learn to honor "who" you are and get more deeply in touch with your authentic self, you will become skilled at trusting yourself.

TRUSTING YOURSELF

Today I trust my decisions and I have the language of self-coaching to support me. I know that when I use my coaching skills to hear what my real needs and goals and dreams and desires are, I am in tune with myself and I can trust in all the actions I take.

When you trust yourself you have created a safe, supportive environment that produces ongoing respect and belief in yourself. This means you are coming from a place of genuine concern for your own welfare and future. Apart from this, you establish clear agreements with yourself and keep promises to yourself. When you trust in "who" you are you will also continuously demonstrate personal integrity, honesty, and sincerity. You will have deep respect for yourself and your personal perceptions, learning style, and personal being. In addition, you will provide ongoing self-support and champion your new behavior and actions. Some of your inspired behavior and actions may include risk-taking and fear of failure, and opening yourself up and allowing yourself to probe into sensitive, new areas.

One of my current clients came to me frustrated after making a business decision he considered his "financial ruin." He was angry at himself and filled with negative talk about himself. As I began to coach him and he began to explore his business decision, he came to realize that he hadn't listened to his gut, which had been telling him all along to not get involved with a strategic partner. What he *did* miss was the trust in his own intuition. In fact, he could only really trust himself when he listened to his inner coach.

COACHING CONSCIOUSNESS

Coaching consciousness refers to your ability to be fully alert and intentional when you coach yourself. To do this you will employ a style that is open, flexible, confident, and effective and will use your sense of humor to keep life light. With confidence you will shift your perspectives and experiment with new possibilities and actions, always trusting your own intuition. You will learn to "go with your gut" and at the same time be open to taking risks. You will exude a confidence that stands in its good stead. True self-confidence is not easily overpowered or enmeshed by the emotions of others.

Often we go through our lives like robots, not paying attention to where we are going or what we are doing. We are not intentional and not fully present. We bump into things, we get hurt, we have car accidents, and we drive without remembering driving. As you coach yourself, always be sure you are fully present and conscious of what process is unfolding for you.

Finally, now that you are familiar with self-coaching competencies, take a moment and reflect on how self-coaching feels.

Are you ready to begin the journey? Well, no time to waste. Begin by incorporating the core self-coaching skills discussed so far in your daily life and, *voilà*, you can answer the simple play-work questions below and claim yourself to be more than a mere sightseer!

PLAY WORK

✓ Which of the skills that you learned so far are you using well?

✓ Which do you need to incorporate more fully into your self-coaching?

COMMUNICATION IS KEY

I am certain you know that good communication is the key to harmony and motivation. Good communication informs, provides dialogue for venting, and makes you feel important. That's not all. As you learn to also make others feel important, they respond positively to you. Well, in this section, you will study the critical self-coaching competencies that make up communicating effectively. The skills discussed are grouped into three segments: active self-listening, powerful self-questioning, and direct self-talk.

COMMUNICATING EFFECTIVELY

The first skill is **active self-listening.** This is your ability to focus completely on what your self-talk is, what you are saying aloud, and what you are not saying. It means distinguishing between your words, tone of voice, and your body language and at the same time summarizing, paraphrasing, reiterating, and mirroring back what you are hearing from yourself and checking in with yourself to ensure clarity and understanding. It is important that you have clarity in the context of your desires, concerns, goals, values, and beliefs. Active self-listening is the ability to understand the meaning of what your inner and outer voices are saying. This ability not only supports your self-expression but encourages you to accept, explore, and reinforce your self-expression. You can thus know who you are authentically.

We typically get so caught up in our day-to-day lives and what is going on in the world around us that we pay little attention to our own inner coach. The inner coach is like a guidance system filled with intuition, guidance, and clarity and knows what the inner "you" really wants and needs. We also don't even hear our own thoughts and sometimes don't even know what we have verbally communicated to others because we are too busy with our constant chatter and the distractions of life. Active listening will change all that and bring you a deep awareness of what you really desire and how much you already know about having what you desire. This will be explained more in the "Tuning In" chapter.

The skill of **powerful self-questioning** is your ability to ask yourself questions that reflect active listening and an understanding of your true perspective. It is the ability to ask yourself questions that evoke discovery, insight, commitment, or action. By asking yourself open-ended questions you will create greater clarity, possibilities, or new learning that moves you toward what you desire. Powerful questions are not designed to justify or probe the past. They will propel you forward.

There will be much more on powerful self-questioning as you get to the chapter "Power Tools for Self-coaching." Know that I never use the word *power* lightly. I do use it intentionally to make you aware of how much of an impact these tools will have on your life.

Direct self-talk is your ability to communicate in a clear and direct manner and effectively reframe and articulate your thoughts to help you understand what you really want or are uncertain about. Direct self-communication means clarity of your inner and spoken thoughts. You must use language that is appropriate and respectful to yourself and to others. Learn the use of metaphor and analogy to help you to illustrate a point or paint a verbal picture that has the greatest positive impact on yourself. The result is to know yourself much better and to achieve integrity with what is in your heart.

We have a stream of both verbal and nonverbal self-talk all the time. Most self-talk is inherently negative; that is how we are programmed and hard-wired as human beings. This can be changed and you will learn to change this as you move forward in self-coaching. Also become mindful of your verbal talk. Are you bashing yourself? Do you blame yourself or belittle yourself? Do you say what I used to say, "I am stupid"? Or do you have some other favorite negative phrase? It is this inner and outer self-talk we will silence as you incorporate self-coaching into your life.

So how is the journey going? It's just the beginning! Are you going on this journey alone, or do you have a companion who is following the book with you so you can learn the skills together? If you are traveling all alone, I tell you that the adventure is more exciting and more thrilling if you share it with a buddy who is also studying self-coaching skills. It is only after you practice with someone real that you can review the skills discussed! Happy hunting!

PLAY WORK

- ✓ Take a moment and think about which self-coaching skills you are using well.

- ✓ Which skills do you need to further incorporate into your life?

- ✓ To whom can you give a copy of this book as a gift so he or she can be your mate on this journey?

- ✓ Go find a coaching buddy to study right alongside you!

Coaching is for Everyone

GOING DEEPER

Now you have reached the end of the first round. No, the adventure is not over. It's just begun. You are simply equipping yourself! The final set of skills presented in this chapter relate to clarifying where you are, creating structure and action, and moving you forward toward specific goals.

The first skill is called **creating awareness.** When you are more aware of whom you are and what you believe, you are able to integrate, interpret, inquire, and accurately evaluate all information for a better understanding of your situation. You are also more aware and able to handle your strengths and limitations too. You will find you are more aware of your own underlying concerns, and perceptions of yourself and the world. This ability will enable you to distinguish between the facts and the interpretation, disparities between your thoughts, feelings, and actions. It will also help you to discover new thoughts, beliefs, perceptions, emotions, and moods which will strengthen your ability to take action and thereby achieve what is important to you. This ability helps to express insights to yourself in ways that are useful and meaningful for you. This is the core competency that helps identify your major strengths versus major areas for learning and growth. Thus, it is of utmost importance to you as you climb the ladder to your personal and career success.

I am reminded of a client who shared with me that he always believed his personal views and opinions were more right than his employees. He wasn't open to hearing their way of doing things or of listening to their ideas. As this shifted through coaching he began to be more aware not only of what they were saying but became open and able to set aside his beliefs and feelings, opinions and emotions and he began to see things in new ways and to learn new things. In six months time his department went from 63% productivity to over 87% and decreased turnover by over 12%. He learned a lot when he allowed himself to become aware of how his own beliefs weren't allowing him to connect to other thoughts.

The skills that help you plan I call **designing actions.** These skills make up your ability to plan and to ponder over a problem or situation and systematically explore specific concerns and opportunities. You will begin to take new actions that will most effectively lead to desired results and deepen new learning. You will also explore alternative ideas and solutions, evaluate options, and make related decisions.

Self-coaching is also founded on **planning and goal setting.** This is your ability to develop and to consolidate collected information and maintain an effective plan that addresses your concerns and major areas for learning and development. Your results will be attainable, measurable, and specific, and have target dates. This ability helps to make you disciplined, planned, and goal centric.

I think what my clients enjoy most about coaching is being able to manifest the life and career they have only dreamed about until now. I have had clients lose huge amounts of weight by using self-coaching (no diet or drugs or exercise); clients find their dream career or start their own very successful business, get with their ideal mate, create much more fulfilling relationships, create an abundance or income, have more love, write music and books, and attract material possessions as well. This is the joy of self-coaching! It is knowing first what you really want, knowing exactly how to have what you want, and, finally, how to take the right steps to get what you want. You will love this part of our journey!

Next we get into **managing progress and accountability.** Your ability to hold your attention on what is important for you, and to take the required action is what I am referring to here. You will develop self discipline and the ability to make decisions; you will learn how to address your key concerns and determine your priorities. You will also learn to take responsibility and be accountable for whatever you say and do.

People who succeed in life generally build on their strengths and ignore their limitations. Each of the above skills enhances and develops your

Coaching is for Everyone

abilities, develops your strengths and makes you aware of your limitations. Until you are willing to more fully understand and accept yourself even with your limitations you can not move on and evolve on your journey to self evolution.

PLAY WORK

- ✓ Meet yourself face-to-face and evaluate your attitudes about yourself.
- ✓ Write down your impressions of what your strengths and skills are and relate them to the core self-coaching competencies.
- ✓ Don't forget to review your learning goals, whether you have achieved them or gotten off track.

"It matters not how strait the gate,

How charged with punishment the scroll,

I am the master of my fate; I am the captain of my soul!"

– Charley Reese

Don't become discouraged because you have limitations. Face them!

Become A Self-Coaching Star

*For I dipped into the future, far as
human eye could see. Saw the vision of
the world, and all the wonder that could be.*

– Lord Alfred Tennyson

W ell, perhaps "star" is a slight overstatement. I am talking about
life's great canvass, about creating the life you desire and deserve. I also want you to understand your role and how you can make ***Coaching Is For Everyone*** count for it's most important participant........you!

By now you should be committed to do what it takes to have and use
good self-coaching skills. While professional coaching is a career, you can
be a self-coach by becoming a person who inculcates all the self-coaching
skills and leads a wonderful life...whatever strata of life you might be from!
To begin with, the first step in this direction is to act with coach-like behavior. That means taking responsibility for yourself and your actions. It means
being unconditionally constructive in interactions with friends, relatives,
and other human beings. It means thinking, **"What do I want to exemplify
as a person who now has self-coaching skills?"** before you speak, act, or
respond. Recognize that self-coaching skills are "learn by doing" practices,
and always practice by living as a coach.

I have an example of how this worked for one of my students. This
student kept having problems receiving email. She sent a rather nasty email

Coaching is for Everyone

to my assistant about how emails weren't getting to her and how it was our fault and was blaming my assistant. She also carried the energy of anger and being a victim. Not very coach-like from a coaching student, right? I picked up the phone and pointed out that the coach wasn't living as a coach and asked the coach what changes she had made in her life from coaching and how many coaching clients she had so far. I was not surprised to find out she had made few changes and thus had no clients—which she also they tried to blame me for. As I coached this student to live and breathe as a coach all the time, she discovered the email problem was with their ISP and sent a loving card to my assistant. She also attracted six coaching clients within the next 30 days. Live from the place of being a coach!

On this journey you can expect to **discover something about yourself you possibly didn't know.** One of the real bonuses of learning self-coaching skills is that you'll tap into talents and strengths you didn't know you had, but you don't find these treasures unless you use them in your life and work. So, just think of learning self-coaching skills as a treasure hunt for and about you! And I know that you will find this journey to be great fun. What? You don't quite believe it can be fun? Here's why it's fun---you get to experiment; you get to make harmless mistakes, and you get to learn to dance with yourself and find that beautiful child-like, happy and free being living within you! What could be more fun?

As we go along **you can choose the coaching stuff you want to practice or the skills that you feel most comfortable with.** This journey is all about you - I am simply your tour guide. You get to choose what areas you want to work and what strategies you want to use, and what feels fabulous for you. So, choose the self-coaching skills that give you the most joy and go practice them. Once you practice them, they belong to you--permanently! **Most important, you just might discover** (and I think you will) **that you are great at self-coaching!**

Here is play work to enhance your newly learned self-coaching skills.

PLAY WORK

- ✓ Two times each day, close your eyes and truly listen to everything you are hearing in your head and listen deeply to your inner talk which is your inner coach speaking to you.

- ✓ What is your inner coach telling you?

- ✓ What have you learned as a result of hearing your inner coach?

Now you are on the right track!

THE IMPORTANCE OF PRACTICE

"Practice makes perfect"...an old saying that stands true for all times to come. If you really want to own these self-coaching skills, you must practice each day. These skills, my dear friend are so intense, have so much depth, that you will not be able to integrate them and make them truly yours without practice. In my experience the only way to fully absorb and digest these skills so they become a part of how you think and how you interact with yourself and others is for you to practice them. Reading them won't give you the integration that you need. Moreover, you get your best self-coaching lessons and hone your instincts with other people so stop reading a while and take a break. Spend time being quiet and hearing your inner coach. Practice this every day and become a person who learns by doing. I can give you all the skills, tools and resources, yet you need to practice to make it all yours. In fact, it is no secret that the first ingredient for success in self-coaching can be summed up in three words.

Coaching is for Everyone

Practice

Practice

Practice

PLAY WORK

- ✓ Every day, practice your self-coaching skills several times.
- ✓ Right now get silent and listen to your inner coach for 10 minutes.

Feeling awkward? Having hesitations? Well, take a moment now to list your hesitations. Those might include things like, **"I'm not good enough, I don't know enough, I'll make mistakes, and I don't have enough time."** However, that is because you are learning self-coaching skills for the first time. I refer to these as blocks. We all have them. Consider them normal and natural. Let me help you get started moving past these blocks.

PLAY WORK

- ✓ List your own hesitations right now.
- ✓ Accept them as part of your learning journey.

Now you might also suffer from a common human condition, that of **trying to be perfect.** Most people new to coaching skills believe they need to be perfect with their skills. This is not the case. I encourage you to **be willing to make mistakes.** Self-coaching is not an exact science and, as you will find, there is no "coaching formula." Rather, self-coaching requires that you trust your own instincts. Since self-coaching is part listening, part responding, and part intuiting, there is room for error. At times, you will make self-coaching mistakes although I prefer to call them "coaching lessons." To become a person who is great at using self-coaching you will need to take enough risks, make mistakes and graciously acknowledge the coaching lessons you receive from those mistakes. In fact, to become advanced using self-coaching skills, you will need to expect coaching mistakes along the way. This frees you from the burden of self-coaching perfection. Go ahead make mistakes and learn from them. **And again I say, "Have fun practicing!"** I promise it won't be the last time you'll be reading those words. Self-coaching is joyful, so feel free to relax and enjoy practicing.

I remember being nervous about listening to myself and wondering what I'd hear. What if I heard that I didn't want to be with my partner or I didn't really like my best friend or I hated my job? It was a bit scary at first. I also recall making many mistakes. I'd try to tune into myself but then I'd get distracted. My mind would wander off, thinking odd thoughts, and I would not be paying attention to myself. One time I stopped hearing my inner coach and began dictating to myself and telling myself my old story of how stupid I was! Yes, I have been on this journey too and the willingness to play and practice and let go will allow you the growth and self discovery you are seeking. Be open! You will not be sorry.

THE TRANSITION TO USING SELF-COACHING SKILLS AND WHAT SELF-COACHING FEELS LIKE

This is a marvelous journey that you are embarking on. It is a significant promise to better you. Like all journeys, however, there will be bumps in the road and detours that will slow your travel. That is, I suppose, true of all major transitions in life. In order to guide your way, here is a road map of what may happen to you and how you may feel along the way.

During the coaching transition, you will move from living the way you are now to creating a new way to live that results in less stress and greater peace. You might get a bit fearful that transitioning to coaching means that you are going to change your lifestyle and while you desire to make such changes they might also be scary. I know this and I appreciate this. For most people this transition is not as simple as they think. The reason is that to be a great self-coach you need to be a great model of a great life. So, you will find yourself improving your life, your work, your relationships and the way you feel about yourself. Those are not small transitions and, sometimes, you will feel overwhelmed. Be patient when the overwhelm phase occurs and have faith in yourself. It will pass.

One of my coaching students told me that she was really excited to begin the journey and then as she made some bigger shifts she got scared. She felt it was too much for her. Other students encouraged her to keep going and to know that this feeling would soon change. When she graduated, she sent me a lovely email telling me how glad she was that she continued to make changes and grow. She said that the life she was now living was her best life because she willing to be uncomfortable. Discomfort causes your growth. Stop being so comfortable!

Accept that you will be letting go of things from the past. As your quality of life improves, you will find that you will put up with less. This will occur in a gentle, loving manner. You will find yourself letting go of draining relationships, asking people to honor your rules and limits, and finishing things from your past. These changes can be stressful while you go through them. It is best to acknowledge that these changes are occurring, that they are stressful, that they are temporary, and that, at the end, you will have a simpler life that serves you well.

I discovered that I needed to let go of some friends that were very nega-tive and this made room for even better, more loving, supporting, and en-couraging friends to flow in. As I said earlier I discovered I needed to let go of my past.

Clients have let go of weight, poor relationships, money issues, past anger and hurt, and given up stress.

Realize that the process takes some amount of time. Developing self-coaching skills is not always easy and it is never instantaneous. It will take longer than you think. Therefore, you must be willing to invest time in your learning and growth, even when both seem to be like a car stuck in a five o'clock traffic jam, going nowhere fast. In addition, you need to be willing to enjoy the journey for the journey's sake. Doing so will allow you to flour-ish as well as to set an example of patience and trust for others to follow.

Understand **that there is likely to be discomfort, chaos, or a feeling of being lost.** Sometimes you will feel that you are not "getting" the skills. Other times, you will feel bored that it is taking a bit too long to grasp. You will get depressed, elated, laugh, cry, and at times, wonder why you ever made this decision to follow this book. Again, all of this is natural. Don't fight it. Wait quietly. Continue practicing diligently. One day, you will simply know you are using your self-coaching skills, with ease, all the time. In my experience I found that I understood the skills logically right away, yet as I went about my day to day life I would forget to use the skills. I kept slipping. The more I practiced, the better I became at using the skills more and more. At about four months into practicing one day I encountered a dif-ficult situation and noticed I didn't fall into my old habit of beating myself up. Instead, I used positive self-talk, came up with solutions and moved on. That's when I knew the coaching was in me! I can't say if this will happen for you in a month, or a few weeks, or in many months; I can tell you that you will get them if you practice and if you believe you have the skills. **Be willing to start the transition by declaring you are skilled at using self-coaching now.**

Coaching is for Everyone

I believe that you were attracted to this book because inside of you is a natural coach. A natural coach is a caring, compassionate human being who loves to hear others and to connect with them on a deep level. He or she is one who is on a life mission to better themselves and to discover their passions and values. These skills are natural to you but may need to be, like a computer disc, reformatted. Other skills may need to be refined. Still other, more advanced skills, will be added along the way. The basics, however, are already there, because you know that you have a deep desire to know your inner thoughts; you want to feel your inner passion and want to live your vision and mission. Because you are reading this, you are prepared to make changes, set goals and create plans. Right now declare that you are skilled at self-coaching and start exemplifying self-coaching behavior and living a coach's life. Your transition will be faster and easier as a result.

Now revisit your commitments to using self-coaching skills. Since you know more about the process, do your commitments need to be revised or changed? Finally, as you go down this road, here are a few wise words from Dr. Seuss to keep your journey joyful and in perspective:

"Out there things can happen and frequently do

to people as brainy and footsy as you.

And when things start to happen, don't worry. Don't stew.

Just go right along. You'll start happening too."

– Dr. Seuss

The Places You'll Go

The Four Foundational
Coaching Skills

The beginning is the most important part of the work.

– Plato

Most people transitioning to using self-coaching skills start that transition with significant fear about their actual coaching abilities. From past experience, I have found that people new to using self-coaching skills are often uneasy practicing coaching. The four foundational self-coaching skills that I am going to discuss here will hopefully alleviate some of that fear, quickly making you comfortable using self-coaching skills.

Now, don't travel fast, skipping the pages won't help you at all! I recommend you take a full week to study and practice one foundational self-coaching skill. Just go through the brief explanation of the skill and then practice that skill for a full week so you begin feeling like you use that skill naturally. The emphasis is on moving you smoothly into using self-coaching skills before you start the more intense and demanding skills. So be prepared to play, absorb, and laugh at your mistakes. I hope that, by the end of this chapter, it will be effortless for you to say, **"I'm good at using self-coaching skills!"**

Halt! Before you speed away, set your goals now by doing your play work.

PLAY WORK

✓ How will I be more comfortable and less fearful at using self-self-coaching skills by the end of the chapter?

✓ Read the chapter because you, my friend, cannot answer this question without reading the chapter... no shortcuts!

THE FOUR FOUNDATIONAL COACHING SKILLS

The first skill is **how to connect with your inner coach.** As you learn these skills you will learn how to quiet your mind and open a space to create an instant connection with what your heart and authentic self desire. Then you will learn the skills of **how to be non-reactive.** You will discover how to remove your judgment of yourself and you will begin to listen and hear yourself from a neutral place filled with self love and appreciation. Then **you will fully get what your inner coach is saying to you.** You will practice retelling what your authentic self is saying and letting it in so you have deep appreciation and understanding of what your inner guidance system is saying to you. And you will learn **how to respond to what you want.** You will learn and practice how to respond by accepting your inner coach and taking inspired actions that feel in alignment for you.

HOW TO CONNECT WITH YOUR INNER COACH

The very first skill you need to develop is an ability to connect fully with what your heart is saying and hear your inner soul speaking to you. Self-connection on this level is something you probably have no idea how to do. We tend to loose this at about three years of age when discipline and rules entered your life and you gave yourself up without knowing it and conformed to what you were told to hear, believe and perceive.

Your inner coach has resided in you since you were a small child and is still within you as an adult. This is the free spirit you have learned to contain by following rules and trying to be a "good boy" or "good girl." Your inner coach includes all your true and deepest emotions, your creative, imaginative and playful side that is trying hard to break free. As we become adults, we push this inner coach down and keep its existence hidden. Your inner coach is right below the surface and often makes you feel uncomfortable when you fear it will come out and are afraid of what people will think of you if it does. Remember the fun, happy, silly child you used to be? Hoping and skipping and playing silly games? That spirit is part of your inner coach and can help you move through your life with more ease and joy and less stress. It is constantly asking to come out and play; it wants to you lighten up and have more fun in your life.

The essence of who you are authentically is still deep inside. It is time for you to open yourself up and create rapport with yourself and compassion for yourself. Befriend yourself as you are the greatest friend you will ever have. When you make this sense of connection you will see how you will trust in your inner coach more and more. Things flow, there is less inner turmoil and you become more peaceful.

As you practice, this instant connection with your "inner coach" (the real you and the silent yet authentic voice in you) will become a natural part of you. In the beginning, however, developing that inner connection means that you must look for your inner coach for the bond to occur.

As I made connection with my inner coach, I found I liked to do fun things. I began spending more time in nature and with people who I could laugh and be silly with. I attracted the most special girlfriend in my life; we hang out and have play dates where we do all kinds of fun things from making silly shoes for each other to watching great movies together to concoct-

ing smoothies and sharing our fantasies. I feel like a kid when I am with her and can't wait to see her. Because of what we do, I now choose to let fun be an integral part of my life now.

It is important that you follow certain "steps" or routines and you practice them so you can connect with your inner coach easily and instantly. The first step is that before tuning in to your inner wisdom, inner guidance, and what I call your "inner coach" you need to quiet any conversations in your mind. When you get quiet and begin to open up to your self particularly for the first time you will really focus on just hearing what you are saying down deep. As you listen to your wise inner coach continue to keep your mind quiet. Don't jump ahead and try to make things happen. Self-coaching is about being in the flow and allowing things to unfold how they do.

Absorb each word and inner thought and respond only when you believe you have fully heard your inner coach. Focus on first hearing your gifts, greatness, strengths, and other positive qualities about who you really are. Do not focus on what you might perceive as negative or wrong about yourself. Respond to the positive. The positive will build up your self-confidence, your success, your day-to-day living—even your health. These are easy steps once they become habits.

PLAY WORK

- ✓ Continue practicing the steps on a daily basis while tuning into yourself and hear your inner coach.

- ✓ Quiet any conversations in your mind before you begin listening to your inner coach.

- ✓ Focus on your inner coach and only your inner coach.

(continue to next page)

> ✓ As you listen, continue to keep your mind quiet. Don't jump ahead. Absorb each word or thought and respond only when you feel your inner coach is complete.
>
> ✓ Focus on first hearing your gifts, greatness, strengths, and other positive qualities. Do not focus on what you might perceive as negative or wrong. Respond to the positive.

HOW TO BE NON-REACTIVE

Hearing yourself without reacting is truly one of the most important self-coaching skills to develop. Hearing yourself without reacting means that you do not respond judgmentally to anything your inner coach might say. You do not think of yourself as right or wrong, at fault or not at fault, or good or bad. You simply "are and your actions simply "are." The basic self-coaching fact is that you do not listen to "fix" yourself, but rather hear your inner coach neutrally to better understand who you are being, where you are, who you want to be, and where you want to be.

If you always remember that you are a child of The Creator, that you are already whole and complete and beautiful and perfect just as you are, even with all your freckles and pimples and lumps and bumps, you will not constantly feel that you need to fix yourself.

Forming opinions quickly will not necessarily be correct and so the outcome or solution you will create will also lack depth and reason. Don't be too harsh on yourself or too biased about yourself. Keep your feelings true to yourself and down to earth; only then will self realization dawn on you. Then, you will know your worth and the course of action to take in order to achieve your aim in life.

Coaching is for Everyone

Letting go of reaction about yourself and self-judgment is difficult. So let's begin your pilgrimage from judgmentally hearing yourself to being neutral as you listen to your inner coach. Begin by quieting your mind of your thoughts before beginning to listen to your inner thoughts. Realize the fact that some of your values and goals might not be in alignment with what your inner coach has to say. Leave yourself and any agendas you may have aside for the duration of being tuned in to yourself. Don't listen to respond to or to satisfy yourself. Instead, you must enter the space of your inner coach and be with this inner guidance. Stop and quiet your mind and refocus when you feel a reaction that is emotionally charged. As a human being, it is important for you to feel, express, and accept your emotions. If you are to feel the joy of positive emotions then you must accept the reality of less desirable emotions too! When your emotions are under control, you say **"I will act the way I feel."** Probably you were a child when you said that. Then people told you that was "bad" behavior. Now I am saying to you, knowing how you really feel inside will allow you to act in alignment with who you authentically are. Choose what attitudes you presently desire to strengthen your inner self, and then let go of attitudes, beliefs, and behaviors that no longer support you. Again don't react, just listen. So hear me out neutrally; don't overcharge yourself, and travel light!

PLAY WORK

- ✓ Listen neutrally to your inner coach for the rest of the week.
- ✓ Quiet your mind often and focus on your inner coach.
- ✓ Hear your inner coach without reacting.
- ✓ Be charge-neutral and non-judgmental to your inner coach.
- ✓ Gain clarity from your inner coach and don't debate the merits of what you heard - just take it in

FULLY GET WHAT YOUR INNER COACH IS SAYING

Reflecting back is an old and time-honored skill in communication. It is where you say back to the person that has just told you something: "What I hear you say is…." and then you repeat back to the person you're talking to what you heard them say. In self-coaching, reflecting back allows you to hear your inner wisdom, to process it, and then tell yourself what your inner coach said to you. This then gives you a chance to confirm what you thought your inner coach said and what the inner coach meant. In coaching terms, reflecting back also gives you the opportunity to hear underneath the actual words or your self-talk and to hear your inner emotions, strengths, a block toward progress, etc. You then have the opportunity to clarify to yourself whether what you heard from inside resonates with you.

To fully digest what your inner coach is saying to you, quiet your mind and focus on hearing your self-talk. Focus on the inner language, the ideas behind the words you hear from your inner coach, and any emotion you feel. Remember to be non-reactive as you hear and then tell yourself what you thought your inner coach said to you and be charge-neutral which means non-judgmental.

Then ask your inner coach whether what you heard is what you really meant. Ask questions to your inner coach like, **"Did I hear that right?"** or **"Is that what you meant?"** Be sure you remain charge neutral so you won't override your inner coach and loose the authentic "you" that is surfacing up through your self-coaching.

Remember this skill is about gaining clarity and insight from your inner coach, making sure you are fully aware and letting in what your inner coach is saying. Allow your inner coach to be heard. It is not about debating the merits of what your inner coach said. As you gain clarity — that essential ingredient required for effective communication — you will be really glad you are tuned in and are returning to your inner authentic self.

Coaching is for Everyone

When I tapped into my inner coach telling me to quit my job, I was shocked and then I realized I wasn't so shocked. Deep down inside I was miserable at my job. I remember questioning my inner coach, but as I reflected back, I had clarity about the message of quitting; I sat down and wrote my resignation letter. Often I reflect on this and believe that if I had not listened, clarified, trusted, and then been honest with myself, I'd still be working in the rehabilitation industry doing something that brought me no joy. Instead I live each day with deep passion for the work I do and for the clients and students I serve. I am grateful I connected to my inner coach. I tuned in. I let it in, and I got clear for myself on my life focus.

You, dear adventurer, are on the verge of discovering many diverse and interesting facts about yourself by reflecting upon your relationships and coming up with self revelations. As you hear your inner coach, be sure to pay attention to your actual self-talk, ideas, and emotions. Hear yourself as a coach would—no judgment, just respect and love. By listening to yourself and allowing your inner coach to speak to you, you will hear what you authentically want and will begin to let it in. In fact you will find your inner coach is very interesting when you become more interested in hearing yourself. As Bob Conklin has said, **"There's no such thing as uninteresting people, only disinterested listeners."** Listen with keen interest to your authentic inner coach.

RESPONDING TO WHAT YOU WANT

Responding is the art of understanding what your inner coach has said to you. As a self-coaching term, responding means that you have heard yourself at a deep level and also makes you aware of the fact that you are now listening to your authentic desires and will live your life in response to what you truly desire and deserve.

Responding to yourself is more art than strict technique. It requires that you listen deeply; fully focused on your inner coach and that you listen with a quiet, non-judgmental mind. This means listening with the heart and then responding from your heart by trusting your self-coaching instincts. The ability to see yourself and love and accept your individuality is the basic attitude that you need to develop to relate to yourself in a loving manner.

Now, because this is an adventure, have some fun practicing responding to your inner coach! The best way to do this is simply find some quiet time, be still, and listen to what your inner coach is telling you. Just sit quietly and notice. Enjoy what you are hearing. Then respond to what your inner coach says. For example, the other night I wasn't sure about accepting a speaking engagement. So I sat quietly and listened to my inner coach asking me if this was an event I would enjoy. I pondered this and realized that it was not what I typically spoke about, so the event might not be a fit. Then listened to my inner coach guiding me to doing things I love more. I responded by telling my inner coach what I really wanted to be doing, and as I had this entire silent conversation I realized I had fully gotten my answer that I didn't want to go to the event!

By doing this reflecting, you can practice responding to yourself in a coach-like way and get to know your real desires. I hope that you are now more comfortable with the idea of self-coaching, using your inner coach! Please keep this sense near as you may be somewhat overwhelmed by what you come across in the next few chapters.

Coaching is for Everyone

Tuning In

Hear me; and be silent, that you may hear.

– William Shakespeare

T uning in to the present is the most basic and yet most critical self-coaching skill that you need to learn. By tuning in, I mean being fully attuned to and present with yourself, honoring, trusting, and accepting your deepest feelings, your true perspective on your life and work.

The most important "tuning in" mechanism is the ability to hear yourself. The ears help you tune in to your own words, tone, emotion, pain, energy, language patterns, and commitment. Through extremely perceptive self-listening you are able to experience what is happening underneath the words. Until you have tuned into all that has been said through your inner coach you can not respond.

The foundation of your loving relationship with yourself that self-coaching is developing is a deeper understanding. You will hear yourself in a new fuller, deeper, more meaningful way. A way that will allow you to tune into the present—to the real person inside you! You will notice several things as you integrate being tuned in to yourself. Most of my clients and certainly all of my coaching students say they first notice many old hearing habits slipping away like shadows. They particularly notice how much of the time they never heard themselves and begin to see this habit changing. I'll bet you will find yourself listening more intently to others as you become more in tune with yourself. This is one of the many great benefits about learning self-coaching, the ability to move from improving yourself to improving your relationships in life.

I was teaching a class by telephone when a student shared that he had been triggered by something his sibling said. This student told us that every time his sibling spoke, the sibling automatically discounted what he said. He said this pattern had been present for years, and he had never believed he could give this up. He shared in this class that he had seen his sibling at Thanksgiving and actually enjoyed being with him. He reminded all of us that we not only improve ourselves when we self-coach, we also improve our relationships with others.

I am certain everyone that as you learn to listen, you will find yourself putting less emphasis on what is being said and greater emphasis on what is meant. You will notice yourself listening to others with your heart and with more openness. As a result, you will find yourself connecting and responding more fully to those around you.

You should know that self-coaching allows you to touch the lives of those around you by demonstrating the cluster of coaching skills that you have been developing and particularly by showing earnestness in listening, sincerity in finding solutions, and by just being there for others. Once you develop skills in yourself, remember these skills apply to all your relationships. I begin with the inner coaching to assist you to be the authentic gem you really are. Once you know your inner being and have connected with your inner coach and are using self-coaching you can thus enrich your relationships, your attitude towards life, and you can make a huge difference in the lives of others. It is then, with these changes that you will take the first major step toward becoming and being great at using self-coaching skills and perhaps these words, written by Stephen Grellet, should become your objective: **"I shall pass through this world but once. Any good, therefore, that I can**

do, or any kindness that I can show to any human being let me do it now. Let me not defer nor neglect it, for I shall not pass this way again."

HOW TO TUNE IN TO YOUR SELF

Let me begin with **how to prepare to tune into yourself.** Self-coaching helps to tune into yourself at a deeper level than you have done. Developing that skill not only takes practice, but it takes preparation. Just as the athlete prepares for a game by wrapping the ankles, warming up the body, and preparing the mind to be on the playing field, you must prepare for the listening game by becoming present, setting aside portions of yourself, and accepting yourself and others.

It is important that you now begin to hear your own behavior patterns. Often a behavior pattern will tell where your energy is being drained. For example if you are spending a lot of energy trying to make things perfect—making sure your home is perfectly clean and your car is sparkling—you might be spending a lot of energy towards meeting perfection. I know in my case, I was spending a lot of energy with friends who were downers. I felt I had to be there for them, yet they were sucking the life from me. You might find that you are being drained by having **your time taken away,** like working at a job you don't like, or doing volunteer work because you feel you have to versus having a true desire to help. Or you may be doing things that you aren't passionate about and spending time not focused on what your real passions are. It is important that you learn to recognize and identify your personal key behavior patterns. As you get in tune with yourself you will also see how **to recognize your strengths.**

Before I tuned into my strengths, I always thought the ability to get up on stage in front of thousands of people was easy and effortless and took no particular skill set. As I tuned in, I began to realize that most people fear speaking and yet I thrive on it. Even as a 5 year old, speaking in front an audience of 500, I never felt nervous. Speaking for me is clearly a natural

strength and something that is inside me and I love to do. Now that I rec-
ognize this, I choose to speak more, and I help others overcome their speak-
ing fears. I know now that just because I accept something I do as "no big
deal," that it could be a "big deal" for others.

If you are like most people you can discern and label your weaknesses. I bet, however, you don't know how to recognize and identify your
strengths—and your strengths are what make you great. When you are using self-coaching skills, in general, you are far more interested in finding and
using your strengths than focusing on your weaknesses. Always remember
this point. It is important to tune into, identify, respond to, and build your
own greatness.

PLAY WORK

Responding to Your Inner Coach

- ✓ Listen deeply focused only on yourself.

- ✓ Listen with a quiet, non judgmental.

- ✓ Listen with your heart.

- ✓ Respond to yourself from your heart, trusting your inner guidance.

THE CRITICAL GAP

In coaching, I often talk about something I call the critical gap. All of us
have this in some way, and in greater or lesser degree. The critical gap is that
large space between where you are and where you want to be. Many times
there is one significant issue that is defining your critical gap. Self-coaching

helps you gain more knowledge of yourself and find out what your gap is. As you get more honest with yourself and in touch with your inner coach, you will learn how to listen to your inner coach and then define your critical gap for yourself. We will discuss this later at a much deeper level. Now I just want you to become familiar with the concept.

*My critical gap has **been** many things at many different times. As I gained knowledge about myself through coaching, I realized my gap was in not having the kind of social life and deep relationships with friends that I wanted. Later when I closed that gap, I realized my gap was not working to my full potential in terms of my professional assets, so I put my focus there. Currently my gap is in financial resources to begin a foundation for children with Reflexive Sympathetic Dystrophy (RSD).[1]*

PLAY WORK

- ✓ Identify your critical gap in tuning in to your inner coach.

- ✓ If your ability to tune in changes for you over the next few weeks what will that change look and feel like.

---

[1] Reflex sympathetic dystrophy (RSD), also known as complex regional pain syndrome (CRPS), is a chronic progressive neurological condition that affects skin, muscles, joints, and bones. The syndrome usually develops in an injured limb, such as a broken leg. However, many cases of RSD involve only a minor, seemingly inconsequential injury, such as a sprain. And in some cases, no precipitating event can be identified.

Pain may begin in one area or limb and then spread to other limbs. RSD/CRPS is characterized by various degrees of burning pain, excessive sweating, swelling, and sensitivity to touch. Symptoms of RSD/CRPS may recede for years and then reappear with a new injury. (Helio Health Library. http://www.healiohealth.com/rsd-reflex-sympathetic-dystrophy-syndrome.html.)

Coaching is for Everyone

As you tune in, always choose to **tune in with your heart** rather than your head. After all love is what makes the world move. I am not referring to romantic or emotional love but love that is the core of our being — the oneness of life. This means that you quiet the noise in your mind and hear your inner thoughts from a deeper, more empathetic space. It is your commitment to yourself to quiet your mind and listen from a place where you truly hear, accept, and understand yourself.

PLAY WORK

✓ Each day practice making yourself right.

✓ Develop a daily hearing theme for yourself. In other words, what do you want the way you hear yourself to say about you? Check at the end of the day and see if the way you heard matched your theme.

✓ Practice listening to your self with your heart and not your head every day.

These skills represent a major shift in the attitude of self-hearing and self-responding that most people possess. Thus, while the concepts are simple, these changes in attitude take resolution and practice and can be expressed daily. Now that you understand more clearly how to tune into yourself, you may have some inner questions. I can tell you from my experience that tuning in to yourself takes a good deal of preparation. You may wonder about this statement. If you are like most people, you assume that hearing yourself and knowing your feelings is automatic, almost a given. You have a silent or voiced thought, the words float through your brain or your ears and into your thought process, and presto - you have gotten your message! Indeed, if all "getting the message" involved was the travel of sound to the brain, the formula might be that easy. Getting to deeply hear your own inner coach, which is what tuning in is all about, consists of much, much more.

Let's look at what happens as you think your thoughts and as you speak them. Tuning in involves the processing of what is heard in the brain by your silent or voiced communication. Think about it. You are looking at the sky. Your inner coach says, "The sky is blue like the ocean." Your brain registers the words. Then, the real listening begins as you interpret in your mind what the words mean. And generally, you will interpret them in accordance with your own beliefs. You will add what you think the blue of the sky is, what you think the blue of the ocean is, and ultimately, you will probably decide whether you agree or disagree that the sky is blue like the ocean and if your inner coach is right. Thus, the real message you get is the conclusion you reach about the spoken or silent words, not just the words themselves. Those conclusions are most often governed by the views and opinions that got layered upon you during your life and work experience and not what your inner coach holds true. Remember that inner coach IS the true you.

When you have your own silent or voiced thoughts, you typically believe what you have thought or said and don't do much concluding. So, the messages you receive you don't really focus on, and you filter them out most of the time. The messages you silently receive really are true for you, if you listen to them. They are your authentic self voice and expression and your true inner beliefs before you changed them to "fit in."

Self-coaching enables you to tune in from a different place and in a different way. You must listen for what your thoughts and words really mean and what those thoughts and words deeply mean to you. Therefore, self-coaching prepares you to hear yourself by removing your own opinions, convictions, beliefs, needs, and wants and clearing that listening space takes purposeful conscious attention. Resolute practice is needed to prepare a clear space so that you can tune into both what you are saying and feeling and what your inner coach means. This clear space is created for you to really hear yourself "being present to your inner coach who is really your authentic self."

BEING FULLY PRESENT TO YOUR INNER COACH

In order to be fully attuned to yourself, you must prepare by setting aside the obstacles to hearing yourself well. We all have obstacles to a clear space and to being present with ourselves. I want you to have the gift of hearing your inner coach with all obstacles removed. When you listen with your own outer trained filters and opinions, you do not hear the truth that your inner coach is speaking. You have these filters which you learned - they are not authentically who you are. You have learned to turn down the volume of your authentic voice and you hear what is interpreted and judged by your mind. In order to be fully present to your inner coach you will need to set aside your ego, your truth, your attachments, and judgments that conclude between right or wrong.

Your ego is your desire to know that you are good. From a self-coaching standpoint, it is that part of you that wants to be told that you are a great person and a high achiever. It may manifest itself by needing to tell yourself how wonderful you are. The "I" my dear friend brings about the lack of listening to your inner coach. You may not want to hear what your inner coach is saying if it doesn't make you feel good about yourself. I tell my clients and coaching students to notice if they are thinking about themselves in the way they are used to being in the world. I ask if they really succeeded in tuning in to their authentic, inside, quiet selves, will they hear what that self really wants. How about you? Are you giving due importance to your inner coach and fully hearing it? Are you clear that you are not responsible for any human being's thoughts or feelings other than your own authentic ones? And are you listening to your inner coach? Let's do some play work to advance your skills!

PLAY WORK

- ✓ Try listening to yourself by first accepting your self and your thoughts as perfect. What did you learn?

- ✓ Identify the three hardest things for you to put aside as you hear yourself. Having done that how did you hear yourself differently than you might have before?

- ✓ Create a great listening space for yourself and be fully present and tuned in. Repeat back what your inner coach said. What did you learn?

- ✓ Continue listening to yourself with your heart.

As you hear your inner coach, be prepared to adjust your truth. We will spend a lot of time on truth in an upcoming chapter so right now just take in the basic concepts. Your truth is what you believe is right. For most people, their truth is an absolute. In other words, it is not only their truth, it is **the** truth. Know that what is the truth for you may not be true for others. Your truth is how you view and interpret factual truth. It includes not only facts, but values, judgments, and emotions and consequently, personal truth varies from person to person. Setting aside your personal truth that you learned and that is not authentic, then, is crucial to becoming attuned to the present and getting to know yourself at a deep level. You have learned to add filters so that when your inner self shares your real truth without you being aware of it, you filter that right out.

PLAY WORK

- ✓ Are you hearing through your personal truth filter?

- ✓ Are you judging yourself or your decisions regularly?

- ✓ Do you beat yourself up for not doing tasks correctly or do you make yourself wrong about information on a regular basis?

- ✓ Are you deciding whether you like or dislike yourself or your actions based on what just occurred?

- ✓ Are you distinguishing between factual truth and personal truth as you tune into yourself?

Answering these questions regularly will assist you in valuing and respecting yourself and hearing what your inner coach holds as true versus your outside self that others built for you. We will visit truth over and over again on our journey so note its significance.

PLAY WORK

- ✓ Hear yourself as you speak out loud. Identify three patterns that tell you where you are and explain what you learned about yourself as a result.

- ✓ Practice simply listening for your patterns without the desire to do more. Simply listen to yourself.

- ✓ Listen with your heart and not your head.

I mention **attachment** to my clients and students in relation to tuning in as well. Attachment is your hope for a certain outcome; it can be emotional or material success. You can see evidence of your attachment when you substitute your self-talk for other ideas that come up, and you try to sell to your inner self that the outer idea is for sure the right idea and the best idea. Attachment is generally a twin of ego. This means that when you are focused on yourself and in the "I" mode you are attached to what you want. For example, when deciding if I'd get value enrolling for a workshop that was almost $10,000, I noticed I was attached to not spending $10,000 and kept thinking things like, "I can't afford it"… "I won't get enough value"… "I don't have the time to go." Attachment showed up and instead of hearing my inner coach I was telling myself what my "I" feared. If attachment inhabits, then you will only interact with the attachment; you'll be compelled to do negative self-talk over your inner coach rather than be fully present to your authentic inner coach.

Due to learned and trained emotional reactions, you will find yourself dominating your self-coach with thoughts and advice, hardly listening to your inner thoughts. You will get a significant personal "high" when you find your outside idea that you forced yourself to believe starts to happen. Inquire of yourself, **"What role am I playing in making things happen and pushing so hard?"** and **"If something completely different happens other than what I have set up, do I mind?"** This will serve in clarifying your attachment or better yet, your lack of attachment. This will allow you to be tuned into your life's journey, nurturing and tending to your self growth. Follow your inner coach and don't let in what your outer voice is selling you.

I learned this as a hard lesson. I wanted to have a sales person and additional teacher in my coach training program. I kept pushing and pushing to have someone show up for this role and was attached to someone showing up by a certain month and date. Someone showed up. My inner coach shouted to me this person was all wrong, and I would have problems if I allowed this person to do sales for me. I was way too attached to the outcome

Coaching is for Everyone

to listen. I told my inner coach to "shut up" and I allowed this person to work in my business. This person nearly destroyed my business with their lack of integrity, and it took me nearly a year to recover. I easily could have avoided this if I wasn't attached to an outcome and allowed my inner coach to guide me. What a lesson! I really got it!

Your judgment is your belief that you are right or wrong. You know when you make a decision and then you think you made the wrong one and you get all over yourself for your bad decision. Or when you praise yourself for following your gut and making a right instead of a left, and you find the location you were seeking because you went the right way. We judge ourselves all the time. How, why, who, and what we judge to be right or wrong is a reflection of who we are and our personal truth. It would seem that judgment would be a natural part of the self-coaching process, but in fact, it is probably the greatest impediment to the process of fully hearing your inner coach. When you judge yourself to be right or wrong, you aren't holding true to your authentic values; you are judging your inner coach and are not open to hearing it with no judgment.

PLAY WORK

- ✓ Hear your inner coach speaking to you. Identify three limiting patterns of behavior and explain what you learned about yourself as a result.

- ✓ Practice listening to your inner coach to hear your patterns without the desire to do more. Simply listen.

- ✓ Practice listening to your inner coach with your heart rather than your head.

You also diminish your personal truth and opinions and come to believe you aren't a worthwhile person. Listen to how you think or speak about yourself. If your thoughts about yourself contain judgmental words, then the way you listen to yourself is probably a reflection of that judgment, and you are not really in tune with your inner coach. I recommend you regularly check your own self-talk and language clues to ensure your judgment is not clouding your ability to be present and in tune with yourself.

One of my nieces, whom I love as a daughter, spends most of her time verbalizing about how unworthy she is. She is constantly on herself about all her faults and mistakes and is filled with self hatred and destroys things in her life through this old pattern. I can only imagine what her inner thoughts are and how harsh and unloving and unkind they are about her. I see her inner and outer beauty, her magic, her gifts and her talents. However, she is the one who will need to see and hear this, and she can do that when she opens to her inner coach who loves her deeply and wants to help her be free of this judgment that she isn't a good person and doesn't deserve to be loved.

Being present and in tune simply means that you are fully aware of your inner coach and your self-talk. Instead of being courteous to yourself, which may sound cliché, practice putting aside your negative thoughts in order to be in tune with your true inner coach. You will feel better about yourself and feel you have connected and heard yourself and are honoring yourself and increasing your self respect. And to truly hear and honor your inner coach, there are certain things you must accept, but before we trudge down that road, here is your play work.

PLAY WORK

- ✓ Hear your inner coach speaking to you. Identify three limiting patterns of behavior and explain what you learned about yourself as a result.

(continue to next page)

> ✓ Practice listening to your inner coach to hear your patterns without the desire to do more. Simply listen.
>
> ✓ Practice listening to your inner coach with your heart rather than your head.

YOU ARE COMPLETE AND PERFECT AS YOU ARE

Since self-coaching is always about you, where you are and where you desire to reach; your attitude must reflect that orientation. **You need to accept yourself as complete.** Yes, complete. You are a human being with your own likes and dislikes, personality traits, value system. You are exactly the way you are supposed to be — and— you don't need to find faults or look down upon yourself. If you learn to accept and embrace yourself as complete, you immediately hear yourself strong, powerful, and ready to move forward. Because once you tune in this way, you will find your own greatness, power, and energy. Positive feelings lead to positive self-communication and reflect progress.

I want you to **believe in yourself.** You are where you are supposed to be and will progress according to your own pace. Don't decide that you aren't in the right place and push to move yourself. When that urge strikes you (and it will), STOP. If you accept a situation and yourself as perfect you will clearly "get" what the situation is telling you and how you can better it to achieve positive results.

A client of mine always put himself down, questioned his decisions and attracted poor relationships and experiences to his life. As I coached him he began to fully accept himself for who he was. He was able to see and feel himself as worthy and began to embrace his own unique personality characteristics. He began to appreciate his skills, abilities, and talents and saw himself as special because of them. Self-acceptance means that we accept that we are each wonderfully different beings and we are supposed to be just that. Personal mastery comes from the self-independence of knowing you are perfect as you are and that all your quirks are just making you more interesting to the rest of us.

Through listening to your inner coach, you can **be sure of your needs, goals, and values.** Life and relationships are always about where you are, where you want to go, and what the best way is to move in that direction. In order to truly tune into the present—where you want to go—and the best way to move in that direction, you must evaluate and accept your needs, goals, ethics and values. Your ethics are your personal standards of right and wrong, good and bad. Ethics are your concern about what you need to do to fulfill what you view as your duty. Ethics help you to determine what is right or wrong, good or bad for you and they allow you to commit to doing what is right and good for you. They include things like being honest, being reliable, being in integrity and being respectful.

By truly accepting your inner coach in these areas, you will hear what resonates for you. Each of us makes different choices based upon our personal needs, goals and ethics because it feels right for us, to get a sense something "rings true" and makes sense. Then I know I am aligned with what I really want to do. I resonate with it and feel no resistance towards it.

I was recently invited to a holiday party, and I suddenly got this sick feeling in my stomach as I pulled back from the invitation lying on my desk. I noticed the reaction and although I typically would go because I thought I "should" I knew that what was true for me was that I really didn't want to go and instantly RSVP that I was unable to attend. Boy that was freeing!

TUNING INTO YOUR HABITS AND PATTERNS

Every one has certain habits that they have learned to repeat over and over again. The habit could be drinking coffee, eating healthy, putting yourself down, or working out. We simply learned something and keep doing it. We have patterns as well. Patterns are ways we respond to the world and decide how to behave in situations. Now, you are probably wondering what habits and patterns you are listening for. I will give you a brief overview of what you will endeavor to hear. You will expand what you hear as you build you listening skills and as you practice your skills.

Let's start by learning to tune into your habits and patterns of conduct. As stated earlier, self-coaching helps to determine where you are and what changes are needed to be made in order to reach your goals for business, life, or both. Self-coaching helps to distinguish your trouble areas and offers assistance in determining the best solutions for you.

Through self-coaching skills, you can gain important information about each of these areas by listening for habits and patterns of conduct. Such patterns often indicate where you truly are, why you are stranded there, what will help you move forward, and what internal qualities need to be considered in determining the next destination. To hear patterns you will need to do the play work in this section.

PLAY WORK

✓ Right now I want you to think about your interaction with work. How do you view your work?

✓ Does it stimulate or deaden you?

(continue to next page)

✓ Are there positive interactions with co-workers or are there confrontations?

✓ Do you talk constantly about work situations or does work seem to be an appropriately balanced part of your life?

✓ The answers to these questions, among others, will allow you to determine where you are in terms of your career and how your business life interacts with the rest of your life.

Another aspect to look at is your **interaction with friends.** Friends are defined as those close associates outside the immediate family and work environment. Close friends are those who support you and are generally necessary for your forward movement. Clues to whether you have those types of friends include whether you speak freely with friends, whether you open up and speak deeply to friends, and whether you talk of their support and guidance. Self-coaching helps to tune into where your current support is coming from in order to determine whether the level of support necessary for you to move forward is available or not.

Another area to considerer is your interaction with money. Whether its business or personal, your relationship with money is often a key factor in the ability to start your journey to a new destination. These skills make you listen to yourself, whether there is a surplus of money, whether you use lifestyle to define self, whether money defines family or business issues, and how money minded or materialistic you are.

PLAY WORK

- ✓ Do you celebrate where you are and who you are or always gripe about what you are not?

- ✓ Do you use words of accomplishment or words of failure when talking about yourself?

- ✓ Does your language reflect a big playing field or a small game board?

- ✓ Simply put, the answers to these questions will allow you to see whether you have a surplus of positive self interaction or whether some surplus of self-esteem might need to be installed.

What I want you to learn from this chapter is that you are whole and perfect and complete. You are a shining bright light and a superstar. You are perfect with all your pimples. Your inner coach knows this.

The outer "you" has simply gotten covered up in the mud of life and doesn't remember your gifts. When you get back in touch with your inner coach and you notice what your true desires are, you can develop habits and patterns that move you forward and surround yourself with an abundance of friends and other support systems. You'll identify what habits and patterns are keeping you stuck and you'll be able to give those up. You'll be back in touch with what is really important to you in life and how you want to live. This is what self-coaching is all about.

So now it is on to more play work to reinforce these concepts for you.

PLAY WORK

- ✓ Hear yourself speak. Identify three patterns that tell you where you are and explain what you learned about yourself as a result.

- ✓ Choose a quiet time each day to tune into your inner coach for the next week.

- ✓ Identify one pattern in each of the areas discussed in this section. What did the patterns tell you about yourself?

- ✓ Practice simply listening to yourself for the patterns without the desire to do more. Simply listen.

Listen to yourself with your heart rather than your head.

TUNING INTO INTERNAL QUALITIES THAT DEFINE YOUR PERSONAL CORE

You are defined by certain internal qualities or ideals that are a critical part of who you are.

This area is somewhat more nebulous than other patterns of behavior and self-coaching skills help to locate the combinations of patterns of being positive as well as self worth and strengths in order to find the clues to these internal qualities.

Tune into what makes you "sing." Earlier I mentioned resonance, which is like a musical frequency that you are tuned to and that feels good to you. Think about what creates energy above and beyond the ordinary. What do you do in your spare time when everyday responsibilities are not attendant? What gives you great joy? The confluence of these elements will assist you in learning about your personal core in a deep and meaningful way. You will use those clues to help in designing your life and career.

I recently had a clue. I was reading an article about juicing. I began to imagine the juice and I could taste the juice and see myself in my kitchen juicing. I could even smell the fresh fruits and vegetables. I instantly pulled the article out of the magazine and the next day bought my groceries and began juicing. I was in resonance with juicing! I didn't stop and tell myself how expensive the fruits and vegetables would be, or what a mess it would be to clean the juicer. I didn't get in my own way by saying I had no time to get to the grocery store. I heard the music that this was right for me and I trusted in that. I am now juicing and loving it!

HABITS AND PATTERNS THAT KEEP YOU STRANDED

Let's now look at the habits and patterns that keep you stranded. I'll start with **the "false-energy" patterns**. Often we have patterns of activity that give energy, but the energy is at a high cost. Moreover, the pattern sometimes becomes so engrained in our life that it is a daily habit that prevents us from moving forward or becomes an excuse for not moving forward. A simple example of such a habit is having a messy office. You may get energy from telling yourself you cannot complete your work due to the condition of the office and yet daily add to the problem by adding to the paper pile.

I kept saying that while I was working a job, I had no time to cook. So every night we had take out or went to dinner if I wasn't traveling. I didn't make progress on my weight loss goals or healthy eating goals and thought it wasn't my fault. I was trapped in the false energy of choosing to eat poorly and making excuses. I spent a ton of my energy coming up with excuses and complaining about poor me and how much I wanted to loose weight. All my energy went to whining about my problem. Until I used self-coaching, I eating badly and whining about my weight. Once I recognized the pattern,

I found ways to have healthy quick foods available in my household all the time and the weight came off!

Self-coaching skills will help you tune into habits and patterns you spend energy on. You will also know if the pattern and energy moves you forward or simply keeps you remaining in the same place. If the latter is true, these skills will assist you in identifying the pattern, recognizing the energy expended, and the detrimental impact of the pattern and assist in building structures to change the pattern.

The next habits or patterns that keep you stranded are your **perceived limitations**. Often people have conversations of failure with themselves. These conversations contain self-defeating or self-diminishing language such as **"If only I,"** or **"I could have done better if,"** or **"If I just did the one additional thing,"** etc. This language will reflect an undercutting of your sense of self on a frequent and regular basis. Self-coaching skills help to tune you into that undercutting and assist you in separating fact from emotion, recognizing what is in your control and what is not, and what accomplishments already exist. These skills will help to retrain the way you speak and think about yourself in order to assist forward movement.

As a human being you will also have   Tuning in skills enables you to listen for your language and self-talk that indicates fear of the new or unknown. One of my clients noticed that they were always worried about the future. They kept wondering what might happen and becoming fearful. After 9/11 they worried about the possibility of being killed by terrorists. When they went on vacation they were worried weeks before if it would rain and ruin the vacation. This is their fear of the unknown showing up.

This language contains allusions to "what if" situations and will often include descriptions of future consequences in exaggerated terms. The language or self-talk may also include references to fears of not being liked, not being admired, and not being right. Self-coaching skills will help you to identify and label fear and create mechanisms to move through the fear easily. Once you notice the fears they actually become less frightening and you'll see less evidence that they are real. I was very scared of climbing ladders. One time I literally became frozen on a ladder and couldn't go up. I asked myself, "what am I afraid of?" and my answer was "falling". I then realized I was about a foot off the ground. Realistically I thought that I wouldn't get badly injured but I had never considered this until I stopped and asked myself what the fear was. When I did I was empowered and went up the ladder! This is how you move through fear. You notice it. You question it. You ask it to prove the evidence or likelihood of it happening and then you bust through it and empower yourself and grow.

Often people **perceive victimization**. These self-coaching skills will help you tune into your language that indicates the belief that responsibility for your present position lies with others. Such language or self-talk will include regular references to the role of third parties or external forces. Self-coaching skills, thus, will help you identify and label your own role and determine what will assist you in stepping into your own power instead of the victim's role.

Once you are able to discern what strands you, you can begin developing structures to remove the stranding habits and patterns. Often, mere recognition of the pattern is enough to start the change. When my client recognized that their fear of being taken advantage of by others was keeping her from making friends. She wanted friends, so she began to see what she feared. She examined her fear of being used and noticed that she had developed a pattern based on her fears. As soon as she recognized the pattern she began to take small actions. Her first action was to notice where she felt like a victim. In one case it was always giving rides to a neighbor's child. She simply asked her neighbor to drive the kids the next day and found the neighbor said "sure." This one step made her feel less like a victim.

TUNING INTO HABITS AND PATTERNS THAT MOVE YOU FORWARD

Just as you have patterns which prevent you from moving forward, you also have habits and patterns that assist you in moving forward. These are not strengths, but instead are habits which create true energy and reflect your personal core. One of these patterns is called **patterns of principle**. You have principles that you live by; these principles are also called *integrity*. Self-coaching skills help you to tune into what these principles are for you and how they are reflected in the way you live. Self-coaching skills will make you aware of how these principles strengthen your behavior patterns. You will also understand how to relate these principles to your current goals and your plans to achieve these goals. Patterns of principle strengthen your ability to achieve your goals.

One of the great benefits of knowing self-coaching skills is that you will recognize your **patterns of being positive** and learn to use language and self-talk such as **"I can," "I accomplished,"** and **"I did well."** When you use this kind of positive self-talk, you will be moving forward with your goals. You will learn how to use past victories to fuel current challenges as well.

Another wonderful pattern to move you forward is called **patterns of self worth**. These skills will help you tune into your thought process. You will be able to judge your true value and worth. You will hear your language of contribution to yourself, community, and family. Language and self-talk that indicates taking account of yourself will be identified and labeled, and you will learn to transfer such ideas to the change process.

An area that self-coaching really serves to strengthen is **patterns of rules and limits**. Self-coaching skills will help you to perceive and set your rules and limits. The distinction between a rule and a limit is simple. You have rules by which you guide your own behavior. An example of a rule is **"I will not lie."** A limit is what you will not let others do to you. It is a protective mechanism that helps to honor yourself and keep you from hurt, or harm, or unpleasantness. An example of a limit is, **"I do not let people use me for their own purposes."** Rules and limits allow you to make decisions easily and to react thoughtfully to situations. Self-coaching skills help you to tune into rules and limits and assists you in determining where strengthening those rules and limits will help you move forward.

I am a big fan of having a simple, easy, and effortless life and I know you will be able to create this for yourself once you tune into your **patterns of simplicity and ease**. Self-coaching skills help you to identify the areas where you work best and with the least amount of struggle. They help to identify why these areas work well and how those characteristics can be transferred to other areas of your life. With these skills you will tune into, label, and assist yourself in transferring to positive behavior patterns. You will be amazed how quickly change will then occur.

Now that you have gathered speed and are truly on your way, here is some play work to tune in more fully to patterns that will help you move forward.

PLAY WORK

- ✓ Get quiet and tap into your inner coach identifying three patterns that move you forward.

- ✓ Choose one time each day to tune into yourself for the next week and listen for more patterns that move you forward.

- ✓ Identify one pattern in each of the areas discussed in this chapter.

- ✓ What did the patterns tell you about yourself?

(continue to next page)

> ✓ Hear one pattern of something positive in yourself every day this week.
>
> Listen with your heart rather than your head.

TUNING INTO YOUR OWN GREATNESS

Your habits and patterns are not the only means for moving forward. One of the best and most important tools is knowing what comes to you naturally. I refer to this as your greatness. It is simply the great person you are—the diamond, the gem with all its imperfections. In order to use your greatness, you must be able to hear and identify it. Existing greatness generally falls into three categories: internal greatness, work skills, and external resources. Tune in and hear the following clues.

INTERNAL GREATNESS

Internal greatness consists of those skills and strengths that you naturally possess. It is the strengths that allow you to navigate life. Often, people are attracted to a person because they want to experience some kind of characteristic that person has. Internal greatness takes many forms. It can include such things as wisdom, energy, courage, willingness, responsibility, humor, serenity, peace, intelligence, inclusiveness, giving, adventure, etc. You have some portion of internal strength that is your true gift.

Self-coaching skills enable you to tune in and identify your greatness and take on that greatness in a new, more powerful way. You learn to widen and spread greatness and begin to employ it as a proactive tool, not just a means to survive. Because the greatness is a natural part of your personal core, it is easily accessed and used. For you to identify your internal greatness, begin to hear what attributes and personality traits of yours attract and connect people. This will clue you in to your internal greatness.

WORK SKILLS

Work skills and strengths fall into fairly discernible categories. These include technical skills, education, professional successes, knowledge, judgment, communication skills, attention to detail, leadership, team ability, etc. In order to tune into your greatness in this area, think about your greatest work successes and how you developed that ability. Begin to identify and incorporate more purposefully those qualities into your professional life.

EXTERNAL RESOURCES

The final area of strengths is one that goes somewhat unheralded: your external resource network. External resources are those people and things that are necessary to your life and work. External resources include everything from a professional network to friends to a banker to a lawyer, etc. You must tap all the resources that can support you in moving forward. Self-coaching skills help you to recognize those resources.

PLAY WORK

- ✓ Listen as you tap into your inner coach and hear your internal greatness, business skills and external resources. What did you hear?

- ✓ Describe your greatest success out loud to yourself. List the greatness that allowed you to achieve your success.

- ✓ Listen with your heart rather than your head.

HOW TO TUNE INTO YOUR CRITICAL GAP

Now that you have explored your behavior patterns and strengths, I can guide you into the critical area of tuning into the critical gap that I briefly introduced you to earlier. The critical gap is the space, large or small, between where you are and where you want to be. Usually the gap is defined by one or more major issues where the gap is quite clear and must be addressed in order to achieve your goals.

A gap is simply keeping you from where you want to go or what you want to achieve. If I wanted to loose ten pounds and have been unable to, weight loss would be my gap. If I never had enough money, finances would be my gap. If I didn't have a partner in life and wanted a relationship, I'd have a gap in having a partner on the journey.

The issues will revolve around internal matters or external matters. It is important to note that there is rarely an external gap that does not have a corresponding internal matter that should be explored. The order in which you explore critical gaps will depend both on what is most critical and what you are ready to work on. To attain this, you have to see yourself as an outsider forging ahead! You have to detach yourself, dissect your behavior, discern abilities, distinguish shortcomings, and develop strengths.

How do you tune into your critical gap? *Just stand aside and watch yourself go by... Think of yourself as "he/she" instead of "I".* These words by Strickland Gillilan very aptly bring out the essence of how to find those critical gap areas and work on them. We are so used to thinking of ourselves as an "I," that even the small shift to "he" or "she" allows us to step away from ourselves and look at ourselves from an outside perspective.

Self-coaching skills help to find out the discrepancy between how much you need of something, internal and external, and how much you have. Self-coaching skills help you to reach beyond and below the words for recurring negative behavior patterns to label what areas you are compensating in.

Coaching is for Everyone

They will allow you to then reach places where you had earlier tried to move forward unsuccessfully. When you put these skills in place they will allow you to break free.

Let's explore **personal critical gaps**. With my clients and coaching students I begin with **gaps in limits and rules**. You may find you have a gap between your limits and rules and will need to create adequate structure to move forward through this gap. Symptoms of this gap may include feeling overwhelm, your inability to say no, your lack of time management, your lack of organization, and devaluing yourself in comparison to others.

I never had enough limits and would say "yes" to projects and opportunities and find I never had enough time to do them. I always felt panicked. I also had a gap in my rules and would allow people to treat me with disrespect and simply take what people dished out which made me feel unworthy.

You'll soon discover how to move through these gaps like I did!

Another gap you may have is a gap **in self worth**. This is a gap between how others see you and how you see yourself. This gap is often characterized by not recognizing your own greatness or value. Symptoms of this gap may include feeling and thinking you are a failure, your lack of belief in your abilities, and your lack of discussion about your strengths. My niece, unfortunately, exemplifies this. She never believes she can do things, or if she does them, she assumes she is doing them all wrong. She doesn't see her gifts and only sees her faults.

A common gap in our society is **in support**. This gap means you either you do not have or have not tapped into the amount of support needed to move you forward. Symptoms may include felling lonely or fearful of being alone, or you feel the lack of a supportive role of others in your life.

I have a client who is a CEO of a very large organization. He shared with me that he feels lonely because he can't share his work experience because he feels the need to always present himself as the fearless leader. At home, he doesn't want to share his financial worries as he knows that would stress his partner. He feels alone, and so he hired me for support to help him find a way to fill this gap.

Many coaching clients and students have **gaps in assets**. This is the lack of internal assets necessary to achieve your goals. Symptoms may include thoughts about you feeling you are "not enough." Also lack of assets can appear in the areas of money, support, love, strength, your ready and willingness, etc.

At a recent workshop I was conducting a young man came up to me on a break and said, "I wish I could study to become a coach but I don't have enough money or time." He is a perfect example of a person with a gap in assets.

The next common gap is the **gap in commitment**. This is your perception that there is a gap in your commitment to achieve your dreams. Symptoms may include a lack of readiness on your part, a lot of talk with no concurrent action, and many ideas without a plan.

I have a really close friend who I adore and who I know wants to have her own business. She's been talking about it for 10 years yet she shows up every day at her job and just keeps talking and talking about how she is going to start her own business. She has a gap in commitment.

Many of my clients and students exhibit a **gap in direction**. If this rings true for you, you will detect that there is a gap in determining exactly where you want to go and what you want to change. This gap is often evidenced by a nagging thought that something should be different combined with an inability to define what should be different. Symptoms may include restlessness without definition and an inability to express what gives you passion and joy.

I had this gap when I was forty. I just felt like I was in the wrong place and nothing made me happy for long. I had dreams and desires, yet couldn't figure out which way to turn to make them happen. Once I got my direc-

tion, not only my career changed, but my relationships, income, weight all changed as well and I found my real joys in life.

Now let's look into your external critical gaps. A most common gap here is a gap in money. If you are in this situation you will discover that there is not enough money to meet your current expenses or to invest in your career. Symptoms include thoughts about lack of money, a reluctance to look at money issues, or lack of profit in your career.

Another external critical gap is in **skill, training, knowledge, or experience**. This is experienced when you don't have the appropriate skill or training to do what you desire to do. Symptoms include a discrepancy between what skills you should have in order to do what you want and what skills, training, and experience are actually present.

And finally let us talk about a **gap in professional assets**. This occurs when you don't have the professional support needed to achieve your career goals. Such support might include a professional network, contacts in a desired industry, money, or advice. Self-coaching skills help you tune into the blocks to moving forward and identify your underlying gap in assets, as well.

Finally, let's take a small respite, a resting gap. As you are on this journey you will notice your own personal gaps and some of these might even be in your learning. You might find you have a gap in being committed to your play work or a gap in practicing your self-coaching skills. This is a great time to notice what your gaps are to learning this material and to self-coaching.

PLAY WORK

- ✓ Identify your critical gaps that block your confidence.
- ✓ Identify critical gaps that block your self-esteem.

(continue to next page)

- ✓ What is the discrepancy between how much you need of something, internal or external, and how much you have?

- ✓ What is your recurring self-talk or recurring negative self -behavior patterns?

- ✓ Where have you tried to move forward unsuccessfully and what, if put in place, will allow you break free?

Coaching is for Everyone

Power Tools For
Self-Coaching

*There are very few human beings who receive
the truth, complete and staggering, by instant
illumination. Most of them acquire it
fragment by fragment, on a small scale,
by successive developments, cellularly,
like a laborious mosaic.*

– Anais Nin

People find their truths about themselves by asking powerful questions. Most people, if they find their truth at all, do so at a slow pace and as the result of unpleasant experiences and lessons. In fact, a good portion of the population spend their lives simply reacting to the present, as if they are characters in a movie, responding only to what is happening around them.

If you recall I mentioned this topic early on and told you to pay close attention to this part of your journey, so student, I expect you to be fully present and deeply tuned in using your best coaching skills to allow in this important information!

For you, I know that you picked up this book because living life by just reacting is not enough. You want to find your truth, whether it is a career truth, a personal truth, or both. You seek to lead your life and conduct your work with purpose based on those truths. Moreover, you do not want to find your truth "fragment by fragment...like a laborious mosaic." Instead, you want to march forward quickly, and to do that, you have come here to learn self-coaching skills.

You are here with this book, so I know you are not most people and you have come to learn self-coaching skills to help you to unravel the truth about yourself. To find your truth, you must step out of always reacting and look at your life from the outside. I know, I've said this before, but it bears repeating. You must be willing to interrupt your typical thought patterns, behaviors, and responses. Furthermore, the purposes of those patterns, behaviors, and responses must be examined.

We use the self-coaching skill of asking powerful questions and making powerful observations and self requests to interrupt or even stop our habit of reacting. Powerful questions are questions you ask yourself that make you stop and dig deep for your honest answer. Powerful observations are things you tell yourself about yourself or your behaviors that are honest and that may even hurt your feelings a bit—they may show off your imperfections. Powerful self-requests are where you ask yourself to do something that is a bit uncomfortable or a bit of a stretch, yet once you challenge yourself, you can then decide if you want to take on that challenge, decline that challenge or compromise, and accept a different challenge.

Powerful questions, observations, and requests are all designed to open you up and get you to go deep into your core with your truth. When you go inside and ask yourself these things you will not only stop reacting, you will "instantly illuminate" a truth. As we march forward you will know how to ask yourself powerful questions, make powerful observations of yourself, make powerful requests of yourself and take powerful actions, thus self illuminating and progressing forward.

As you may have noted, I am using the word "powerful" frequently and this, my friend, is done intentionally. The questions and observations and requests we typically make of ourselves are only informational in nature. The informational question or observation or request is designed simply to elicit further information that may or may not ultimately be useful to our self growth and evolution process. The powerful question, observation or request is not intended to be informational. Instead, it is intended to help you look at a situation differently, look at yourself differently and to assist you in clarifying the purpose of your actions, or to propel you forward quickly.

Some of the important aspects in this chapter are that your questions, observations, requests, and actions will become more focused. You will find your purpose of current actions and your observations will reflect a truth that you may not be aware of. Further, self-questioning, observations, and requests will move you forward at an astonishing speed, and you will understand the power of these skills, not by asking the most difficult question or making the hardest observation or giving yourself the largest challenge, but just by noticing how your responses impact your life. It is everlasting and enriching!

Powerful questions, observations and requests are based on asking yourself or telling yourself something you have not before. Once you are deeper into understanding yourself based on what comes up for you as a result of using this power tool you will then move into actions aligned with what you have learned. I am sure you wonder how to know what questions to ask, or observations to make or requests to make of yourself, just as my clients and coaching students do. I say to them, "get in touch with the most important things you feel and hear each day. Then ask a powerful question of yourself or make a powerful observation of yourself or make a powerful request. Just tune in and you'll know what feels right." Remember that we are using these power techniques to help you create positive solutions for your life and work. I'll be giving you the exact way of doing this in just a bit.

PREPARING TO BE POWERFUL

In order to ask yourself a powerful question, make a powerful observation or make a powerful request of yourself you must be fully in tune with where you are and where you want to go. In other words, it is absolutely essential for you to be fully oriented around your inner core for powerful tools to be used and a powerful result to occur.

You have to think deeply, hear your own tone, notice your emotion and behavior patterns, and be aware of your strengths, to know what lies underneath—to know your very inner essence. All these are integrally related. For example, you may recognize a behavior pattern that is out of alignment with your core; perhaps you begin to feel like this behavior isn't right for you any more. For example, I wanted to be healthy, but I was drinking a pot of coffee every day. I realized this behavior pattern was not aligned with my deep inner desire. Thus, the most powerful question you may ask yourself is "**What did I hear from my conscience and how far away am I from being true to myself?**"

Powerful questions, observations and requests, if asked earnestly and sincerely answered, will often generate a powerful response. They might create great emotion within you or even great chaos in the way you view your world. They may require substantial action, or promote significant thought. These power tools should elicit a notable reaction from you. You must therefore be centered in your skills and detached in your attitude. You cannot be attached and at the same time allow and find your true reaction. Before every such self analysis, be clear that you are ready for any reaction and can respond in a way that will support and assist you to move forward.

PLAY WORK

✓ List four commitments to upgrade your self-talk to be a powerful self-coach.

(continue to next page)

> ✓ List four ways you will practice asking yourself powerful questions, making powerful observations, and requesting powerful actions over the next four weeks.
>
> ✓ State three learning goals you will achieve over the next four weeks.

THE CHARACTERISTICS OF POWERFUL QUESTIONS, OBSERVATIONS AND REQUESTS

Just as there is no coaching formula, there is no formula for developing your powerful questions, making your powerful observations and asking yourself powerful requests. Powerful questions, observations and requests do, however, have precise characteristics. **A powerful question, observation or request always has a purpose.** The purpose is to unfold your knowledge of a situation and what that tells you about your present position and where you want to be. You will use the tools of powerful questions, observations and requests to tap into your barriers or strengths, to know what you need to possess in order to move forward. Each of these tools comes from your desire to know what the most important thing is that you can do to create a path to forward motion and to create that motion now.

An additional point I want to make here is the distinction between powerful questions and powerful observations. Powerful questions assist you to get to your truth and then tell the truth. Powerful observations are the mannerism, the thoughts, and the situations relaying the truth. Thus, a powerful observation comes from your deepest inner point of view. Therefore, you must be ready and willing to own up to what you observe as your inner the truth, even if it is not to your liking! **A powerful observation is always truthful.** It requires you to be absolutely truthful about what you see, feel or hear. It means you must be willing to be at risk and be bold enough to face the absolute truth about yourself. Also **a powerful observation is not about you being right.** Because a powerful observation is about you and allows you to learn more deeply about you from the inside out, you should be absolutely sure that the observation is not simply your opinion, but "the truth." Therefore, you must learn to accept that you need not be always right and you may find out a lot about yourself by going deeper and not fighting your inner coach even if at first you don't agree with it. Further the observation should not be your rigid judgment but a flexible device to move you forward. Another point about a **powerful observation is that it will often enhance your focus on issues and your awareness of your "critical gap."** You may find identifying the nature and size of the critical gap is somewhat problematic. Often, this is because you do not truly recognize where you are and what issue is creating your gap. A powerful observation in this area can assist you in rapidly identifying what must happen for your gap to be bridged and help you to focus on a particular issue or characteristic that is critical to your progress. By making an observation about your key strengths, challenges, fears, opportunities, etc., you can, with the help of your newly found self-coaching skills, make rapid progress in these areas.

As an example, I asked myself this powerful question after I ruptured my Achilles and allowed myself to gain a lot of weight, "Terri, why do you choose to be overweight?" I knew I had tapped into to something powerful as I actually found myself getting angry with myself and starting to defend the word "choose" and to blame others who were making my meals and to say it was due solely to lack of exercise. It woke me up. Two days later I started a 20 day juice cleanse and kick started my weight loss.

I also just made another powerful observation that I want to share with you. Just recently, I found about a program that I want to take a program that costs $30,000, but I just spent that exact same amount on another program so I told myself I couldn't do it. Then I made this observation, "I think *you are withholding the program from yourself as the first $30,000 program was a complete flop and you fear this one will be, too." Yep, that was right on! Observing this helped me change my thoughts and my action instantly.*

Also, **a powerful observation provides a strong foundation to grow, change, and move forward.** Because a powerful observation helps you to focus on particular issues or define your critical gap, the observation creates a space where you can identify changes that need to be made and actions to create those changes. You can also relate the actions to who you are and who you want to be. This provides a powerful arena for the illumination of truth, the application of that truth, and the forward movement that truth begins.

You will do these steps quite quickly in your mind and while they will seem to happen, simultaneously, it is important that you are aware of your thought process. That awareness enables you to build your self-coaching skills and keep questioning yourself.

Each power tool is **present-oriented with future implications**. The powerful questions, observations and requests help you learn more about how you see yourself, where you are, and where you want to arrive. Thus, when you use a power tool they will help you to identify and label your current situation while helping to develop an answer that will push you past the present moment. **The power tools make you see differently.** You are often reacting to your life and work instead of proactively planning and living them. Much of that reaction is a reflection of your habits, behaviors, or thought patterns developed over many years, almost a belief that "this is the way it has to be." Self-coaching thus helps you to step outside being reactive and see things differently. **A power tool helps you to face the truth.** You have come here to know the truth about yourself. Many times, you suspect the truth, but are afraid to voice it because it may mean undertaking significant change. In fact, often the reason behind asking a powerful self question or making a powerful self observation or making a request of yourself is to hear yourself speak the truth without judgment. **Each power tool helps to separate facts from interpretation.** You have filters through which you process information. Those filters include your perception, emotion, desired outcomes, needs that must be met, etc. Sometimes, the filters take information and reconfigure it in your mind, giving it an interpretation that is personal, but not always a reflection of factual reality. Each power tool can help to identify these filters, how those filters have altered facts, and assist you to see factual reality rather than the perceived reality shaped by your own interpretation.

A power tool generally elicits an answer, forward movement, and concordant energy and action. Rarely will one of these tools simply create a brief thought or answer from you. They get you to begin to move forward. You find new energy and begin new actions. A power tool almost always creates a vibrancy which did not exist before. Human being alone, of all life has been given the gift of thought. That is your most cherished possession---the ability to choose your thoughts. Self-coaching skills will help your thoughts to be based on what your real answers are, what is really true for you and what you are really committed and willing to do with your life and work. Power tools are thought provoking and action oriented!

Using the power tools takes preparation, understanding, and practice. You now know how to prepare. You understand the characteristics of the power tools. And to practice them know they are designed for you to think deeply about the situation or about yourself and what it all means to you. You get clear from your heart on what you have seen, heard or felt that might be important to the matter. Finally, you use a power tool that will have meaning and context regarding your situation. Do so as a separate entity without coloring it with your opinion or judgment that lives outside of your inner coach.

I hope you are now noticing that you are no longer a stranger to the land of self-coaching but have become friendly with the surrounding! Wear your thinking cap and review your play work on a regular basis and see if you are living those qualities and attributes. Are you acting more like a self-coach?

If this is so, then this calls for a celebration! If not, use the techniques you learned to help close your critical gaps and address any issues. After all, this journey is for you, and so I encourage you to ask powerful questions of yourself, to make powerful observations of yourself and to request powerful actions of yourself.

Get going! Take the power seat! As you find power, here is your play work.

PLAY WORK

- ✓ What is the most powerful question you are willing to ask and answer for yourself?

- ✓ What is the most powerful observation you are willing to make about yourself?

- ✓ What is the most powerful request you can make of yourself?

- ✓ How can you use these to improve your life?

- ✓ Each day for the next several weeks, identify one truth about yourself and ask yourself a powerful question about it.

- ✓ Each day for the next several weeks, identify one truth about yourself and ask make a powerful observation to yourself about it.

- ✓ Each day for the next several weeks, identify one truth you hear and make a powerful request of yourself about it.

Coaching is for Everyone

Building Yourself

All experience is an arch to build upon.

– Henry Brook Adams

Often in situations that are not to your liking, you find yourself with defeating self-talk, lingering self-doubts, and a relatively small view of who you are. Now self-coaching helps you to recognize the greatness in yourself, and it helps you to recognize your greatness by yourself. Self-coaching skills allow you to communicate your greatness and know that it is not puffery, flattery, or insincerity because the skills enable you to see the truth about yourself and to acknowledge and honor who you are. You naturally see the best in and desire the best for yourself, instinctively at the same time begin to believe more boldly and fully in yourself. Thus, self-coaching skills will assist you in discovering, embracing, and growing the very best within you. I refer to this process as "building yourself" because we have all been knocked down, beaten up and told we weren't near as beautiful as beings are we truly are.

"All that Adam had, all that Caesar could, you have and can do....
Build, therefore, your own world."

– Ralph Waldo Emerson

Coaching is for Everyone

As you build yourself, you not only will you build your inner person, you will begin to allow that inner person to create the life you desire and deserve. Knowing how to build yourself will give you skills that will bestow a whole lot of wonderful attributes in your life that will surely enrich you as a human being. You will innately begin to look for and find your strengths. You will stop looking for your faults or things to fix about yourself and you will stop judging yourself and start appreciating the wonderful uniqueness of who you are. It is time for you to begin to absorb your gifts and learn lessons you need and to begin to hold a larger view of who you are and what you can do.

YOUR "BUILDING" BLUEPRINT

Self-coaching skills of tuning into your inner coach, hearing your critical gap, asking powerful questions, making powerful observations and requests and learning about your habits and patterns help to build a number of things. The skills you have learned help you to build trust in yourself and in your relationships, and to build structures that help you to achieve your goals. They also give you better communication skills.

Your self-coaching blueprint thus refers to the use of your new self-coaching skills to discover, embrace, and grow the very best of who you are. In more basic terms, the building blueprint consists of skills to increase your level of self-awareness of your positive attributes and characteristics. It is the process in which you step into your own power and strength and do so joyfully.

You may be asking **how building or rebuilding relates to self-coaching**. You have some degree of negativity about yourself. It can appear in defeating self-talk, the **"I can't," "I've never been able to,"** or **"my weaknesses are."** It is also evident in your behavior patterns that prevent forward movement. Conversely, you spend far less time appreciating who you are, what you've accomplished, and what your strengths are. Because your view often emphasizes the negative rather than the positive, that view can impede both your vision of your future and your ability to move forward.

This is where self-coaching does miracles. The self-coaching skills assist you to reclaim your positive self. As you begin to reverse negative conversations and thought processes and replace them with a capacity of confidence, your vision of yourself and your journey begin to clear. Negative blocks become smaller and disappear. Energy spent on self doubt evaporates and becomes energy spent on forward movement. Forward movement becomes easier and more natural. In short, building skills allow you to build self-image and build your future. You will also learn how those skills can be used to build trust in yourself and faith in your own ability to journey forward. Above all these skills will teach you how to recognize what innate strengths exist, and the value and use of those prior strengths. You'll understand your personal history, experience, and have a greater sense of self to achieve what you want and will finally end up accomplishing your goals. In this building process, you also gain some invaluable rewards such as greater self-knowledge, a positive view of who you are, elimination of self-doubt, elimination of defeating talk and behavior patterns, more energy, a clearer view of life, more possibility, more peace, greater confidence in the future, and more fun!

WHAT SKILLS DO YOU USE TO BUILD YOURSELF?

In order to build yourself, you must start with the foundation for building. That foundation includes clearly acknowledging and recognizing who you are and what you want. Understand that where you are now is precisely where you are supposed to be, and that the present has innate and powerful lessons that should be recognized and internalized. Focusing on and working with what attributes and assets you already have and identifying and using your natural strengths are all part of how to build you.

Coaching is for Everyone

Each of these skills plays a significant role in building you. By the end of this journey, these skills will be an integral part of your self-coaching skill set and you will use them easily and without struggle. To hasten that process here is some play work to help you.

PLAY WORK

- Describe your own strengths, experiences, who you are, and your unique gifts.

- How can you use these to improve your life?

- List three habits you must change in order to see your strengths rather than weaknesses around you.

- Tell yourself your strengths, experiences, or gifts.

- Two times a day stop and acknowledge and appreciate yourself.

- Once a day be quiet and see how the moment is precisely what it is supposed to be. See what you're supposed to learn.

THE "BUILDING" FOUNDATION

As you tune into yourself, you will begin to hear what exists and what is missing in your view of yourself. In this section, I will describe the essential "building" foundation that you need to identify and which will then help you secure this foundation in your mind so that true forward momentum can begin. Additionally, the foundation provides a solid place to return to when there are collapses in the building process.

To build yourself doesn't mean you are broken or need to be fixed. It simply means that the inner authentic you has been hidden and you are allowing that person to show up. You do this by recognizing **who you are and what you want**.

PLAY WORK

- ✓ Recognize who you are and what you want.

- ✓ Understand that where you are now is where you are supposed to be, and the present has innate and powerful lessons that should be recognized and internalized.

- ✓ Focus on working with what attributes and assets you already have.

- ✓ Identify your natural strengths.

In order to have a surplus supply of confidence and faith in yourself, you must first understand who you are and where you want to go. This includes identifying your key values that are integral to happiness, to when you are most satisfied. You need to know what you really enjoy doing and how "doing" relates to your happiness. Thus you can determine what changes will increase your happiness and success. When you have identified these basics, true building can begin.

In my work with clients and my coaching students, I hear typical human complaints about the present not being right. I think I've heard them all, and I am certain you have many of the same complaints. Do you feel like you just don't have enough time? Do you feel you don't have enough money? Are you having poor relations with family or co-workers? Do you feel un-

Coaching is for Everyone

happy with your work or do you have a business that is not growing as you would like it to? And the big one—do you feel stressed?

Complaints like these are part of the way you look at the world in the present. You notice your present experience and only see and what is wrong with that present. **And your complaints about the present block your view of your future**.

Through self-coaching you will see what the present is about, and what is right about the present. Your self-coaching skills will help you not only to perceive what the present is about and what is causing the dissatisfaction but also label the causes of dissatisfaction, and further, those causes can be eliminated and you can move forward.

Self-coaching skills will also help you to see what is right about your dissatisfaction. In general, the common complaints about the present reflect an underlying relation between action or attitude and result that you have not yet learned and/or absorbed. Because the message has not yet been learned or absorbed, you repeat actions which create dissatisfaction. By learning self-coaching skills you will identify and absorb these lessons on actions, attitudes, and results, and you will integrate the lessons into your life permanently, thereby eliminating defeating behaviors. Once you learn how to identify and label such lessons, you naturally begin to turn your energy to forward movement rather than repeating behaviors and attitudes that keep you blocked.

PLAY WORK

✓ Listen deeply and differently to yourself three or four times a day.

(continue to next page)

✓ Wait to respond to yourself talk until your inner coach has completed its thoughts.

✓ Wait to respond. Think about what your inner coach just said to you.

✓ Ask yourself what the most meaningful question is you can ask yourself and then ask the question. Do not assume you know the response or that you know what the response should be.

✓ Ask the question in simple language.

FOCUSING ON AND WORKING WITH ATTRIBUTES AND ASSETS THAT YOU ALREADY HAVE

Without being conscious of it, you often focus on what you lack rather than what you have. As a result, forward movement is often blocked by these perceived "lacks." Self-coaching skills help you look for what you already have in place to use. These include physical assets such as money, time, current staff, supportive relationships, etc. In addition, these skills identify intangible assets such as creativity, imagination, resolve, attention to detail, etc.

This change of perspective helps you develop the habit of being confident in the tools already at your disposal. As a result, you artlessly begin to build your belief in your possibilities. This self-building becomes an impetus for forward movement.

PLAY WORK

- ✓ Listen deeply and differently to yourself three or four times a day.
- ✓ Wait to respond to yourself talk until your inner coach has completed its thoughts.
- ✓ Wait to respond. Think about what your inner coach just said to you.
- ✓ Ask yourself what the most meaningful question is you can ask yourself and then ask the question. Do not assume you know the response or that you know what the response should be.
- ✓ Ask the question in simple language.

HELPING YOU IDENTIFY AND USE YOUR INNER STRENGTHS

Along with focusing on "lacks," you also frequently focus on what are perceived as weaknesses. You, however, have innate, or inner, strengths. Those strengths have allowed you to accomplish everything that you have so far achieved. Those strengths, however, are rarely the center of your attention.

Self-coaching skills help the process of enumerating your abilities and powers. After you have clearly identified and accepted the strengths that have brought you to this point, you start to build those strengths and use them as tools to build your future. You will thus change your view from what hasn't happened to what can happen.

A woman attending a corporate workshop told me about why her job was stressful and why she wasn't going to get promoted to the job she really liked. She told me her faults quite freely, and they were plentiful. When I asked her about her strengths and coached her to dig for them she shifted her energy and noticed more about herself and the possibilities for her expansion on her strengths. She told me I was brilliant, and I had to laugh. She was the one that did all the work!

Remember, success is a journey and not the destination so don't be disheartened or lose patience, just keep going. In order to help you to further, however, it is important to take a moment to understand that what you have done up to this point is very powerful and very great. You need to dwell a little bit on your successes, and enjoy the process of acknowledging yourself as you do the following play work.

PLAY WORK

Ten Exercises to Illuminate Greatness

- ✓ Write a story about your three greatest successes.
- ✓ Create a list of your ten greatest accomplishments and what you had to do to achieve them.
- ✓ List 10 ways you have contributed to the lives of those around you in the last month.
- ✓ Keep a journal of the little things you do everyday that serve yourself and others.
- ✓ Keep a list of compliments that others give you for 30 days.
- ✓ Think of how much you have accomplished to date and write what characteristics, skills, and strengths have brought you to this point.

(continue to next page)

Coaching is for Everyone

- ✓ Each morning, write down what you deserve out of the day. At the end of the day, check and see if you made it happen.
- ✓ Ask 10 people what they like or love about you and why they keep you in their lives
- ✓ Write a story about yourself that explains why you like being you.
- ✓ List five great things about your spirit that you would like to express every day.

Growing Yourself

Growth takes place when a person has risked himself and dares to experiment with his own life.

– Herbert A. Otto

You are about to enter the self-coaching realm of experiencing growth within yourself. It is a realm where, with care and compassion, you will experience tremendous progress and development. It is where excitement is created, momentum is built, and energy is sustained. It is growth made real.

Self-coaching skills help you to change and attain different results. As in the words of Thomas Crum, **"Being willing to challenge yourself allows you to move from a point of view to a viewing point -- a higher, more expansive place."** Real differences in results come from tangible and meaningful work and happen when you do more than what you thought you could. Growing skills will help you to create space and structure where you can do more or can test your own beliefs and assumptions or think in a new and perhaps completely different way. It is the self-coaching skill of sensing what you are truly capable of doing or thinking.

I didn't think I could begin my own business and be an overnight success, nor did I think I could become a bestselling author or at the top of my profession. That was until I discovered what I was really talented at.

Coaching is for Everyone

I thought myself as small, and so I lived small. Self-coaching shifted my life completely!

These self-growing skills will enable you to do much more than what you thought you were capable of. And they will challenge your old beliefs and turn your new ideas into action. As you practice these skills, you will notice important effects. You will develop greater self-confidence and belief in your own capabilities and ability to achieve. You will create new possibilities and new ways of thinking. You will create energy and freedom as well as forward movement.

You are already aware of who you are and what you want to be, but you need to learn how to 'be there' and how to gather confidence and accept challenges. These growing skills will help in your growth and help you re-examine your long-held beliefs with compassion and power. Often, you do not understand and have not made the real commitment needed to achieve your goals. These skills will help to identify your true intent and help you achieve far more than you thought possible.

ENHANCING YOUR INNER BEAUTY

As you begin to get a clear picture of who you are then you will know more about where you want to be and you will begin to know what you are capable of doing. You will then begin to expect more from yourself. This ability to build increasing trust and confidence in your own abilities, while challenging your own self, requires that you are a person who is charge-neutral. This means that you do not get emotional energy from the progress or lack thereof. In addition, charge-neutral means that you will not be judgmental of yourself.

Often, despite good effort, you may not be able to complete an assigned task. Just do more than you thought and be ready for the next hurdle. Moreover, sometimes a task will cause you to realize that the goal you thought you wanted wasn't the right goal for you. So, while the main challenge will remain undone, you will have made substantial progress. Thus, you may use the skills to think differently and in a manner that will best help you grow. These self-coaching skills give you the freedom and the confidence to follow new paths, and you will be willing to experiment with life and to try many new and daring things simply because no one is going to judge you, not even yourself!

In order to create the trust necessary to grow, you must incorporate a certain spirit and demeanor into your personal core. Do not measure your worth by successes or failures. You are not trying to fix or make yourself "better" but you are enhancing what you already possess. You must not be judgmental of yourself. Instead, give total freedom to your inner coach and start thinking differently in a manner that will best serve your purpose. Be unconditionally positive about any outcome.

If you can incorporate these attributes as a natural part of your self, it will be easy for you to re-evaluate your assumptions and ways of thinking. More importantly, it will be easy to change your thinking pattern as you engage in this growth, and your progress in all spheres will be enhanced.

Dying to begin? Start by incorporating these attributes into your life and whenever you find yourself judging yourself by success or failure, stop for a moment and ask what that "charge" is telling you about yourself. See your judgment and question it.

PLAY WORK

- ✓ List four changes you are willing to make in order to ask yourself for more.

- ✓ List four ways you are willing to ask yourself for more over the next four weeks.

Coaching is for Everyone

BASIC SKILLS FOR SELF-GROWTH

Get ready, as the self-coaching skills I will reveal to you from this point forward are a little stronger, sometimes a little more extreme, and a bit more serious. I will start with three basic "growing" skills. These skills are first to identify the actual intent and resolve, expand the goal, and assign tasks. Again, however, a reminder - like all self-coaching, there is no formula. Therefore, do not use these skills as a routine or in a certain order. Listen to your need, absorb, and respond with what is appropriate in the moment.

IDENTIFY YOUR ACTUAL INTENT AND RESOLVE

Often, you fail to identify the intent behind the change you want to make or the commitment it will take to change, achieve a particular goal, or both. Self-coaching skills assist you to identify your underlying intent or what you want from change. It also helps you to identify what resolve you must make in order to achieve what you want. In order to do both, you must do some self-questioning and observation.

PLAY WORK

- ✓ Answer these questions to identify your actual intent and re-solve around an important goal for you.
- ✓ Identify an important goal.
- ✓ What will I get if I achieve my goal of _____?
- ✓ How would my life be different than today if I achieved this goal?
- ✓ What is standing in the way of my ability to achieve my goal?

(continue to next page)

- ✓ What are the three most difficult things I am willing to do to achieve my goal?

- ✓ What is the hardest thing for me to do now?

- ✓ How do I have to think differently about this to move forward?

- ✓ Identify what you say versus what you do and what the difference signifies.

- ✓ Notice your behavioral clues that indicate your lack of commitment.

- ✓ Observe the decisions you take and whether they are congruent with where you want to be. Thus you can focus on what your actual intent and resolve is.

EXPAND THE GOAL

As stated above, meaningful change comes from meaningful work. The most worthwhile work is usually achieved when you do something you're not certain you could. The dimension of the accomplishment makes it valuable and compels you to believe and that you are bigger and better than what you originally thought yourself to be. This theory underlies the skill I call "expand the goal."

I first had a goal of becoming a coach working from home in a quiet little business. Later I began to see that having a coach training program was part of that business, and I expanded my business goal for that. I then realized that I wanted to give keynote addresses, seminars, and workshops as well as coach groups of clients, write books, and make informational and self-improvement products. I am expanding the goal right now by making a

Coaching is for Everyone

TV commercial next month! This is all a pretty big expansion on the goal of "I'll coach a few clients from my home"!

The steps to expand the goal are simple. First you determine an appropriate goal, and then you expand or enlarge the goal significantly. For example, let's say your goal is to make $10,000 more. You may consider a larger goal of financial independence. Of course, you are at the liberty to reject, or modify the expanded goal. The keys are that the expanded goal is doable but challenging; it is related to and comes from your own goal. So, as the saying goes: shoot for the moon; at least you will end up with a star. Thus, expanding the goal allows you to immediately think larger and your horizon widens.

ADVANCED SKILLS TO BUILD YOURSELF

The last three skills you'll learn in this chapter are unusual. One requires a velvet touch; the other two a sense of play from you. The first requires you to look at where exactly you are positioned in terms of your self-knowledge when there is something huge in the way of you trying to progress or where you have to make a tough decision, or where you have to think more broadly about how your goals interact with life. The self-coaching skills you'll learn are to identify the heart of the matter (the one that requires the velvet touch), ask for the why, and change your viewpoint.

IDENTIFY THE HEART OF THE MATTER

Often when you are very personally attached to the outcome of what is happening; you are unable to see the reality. In these circumstances, you often ignore, or can't perceive, that there are one or two significant issues that must be addressed immediately, or that there is a significant decision that must be made in the very near future. Self-coaching skills help you to identify the matter by helping you to take a detached view, set aside your emotion, and take a second look at the situation from a more dispassionate place. This ability to move away from your emotions and to face the facts of a situation allows you to get to the heart of the matter. And thus you can then begin to solve the issue or make the tough decision in a more open frame of mind.

Getting to the heart of the matter is difficult. It often requires giving up a long held goal or belief that just does not work any longer. This can be emotionally tough, but it is critical for you under such circumstances to remain detached, confident, and positive about the outcome.

PLAY WORK

- ✓ Validate your response to your inner coach's question as being your inner truth.

- ✓ Listen deeply to how you describe your world.

- ✓ Wait to respond to your inner coach until you are sure you heard all that your inner coach has to say.

- ✓ Wait for a moment to respond. Think about what you heard and what it means to you.

- ✓ Decide what you have heard from your inner coach that might be important to you. Make an observation you think will have meaning to you. Do so without being attached to whether you will accept the observation or act on it.

- ✓ Make the observation in simple language. Do not use the observation to imply that you are wrong, have made a mistake, or that you are judging yourself.

Coaching is for Everyone

ASK FOR THE WHY

This is an easy, but highly effective skill. Sometimes, you have goals just to have goals without having fully thought through why the goal is meaningful. Sometimes you are stuck on a thought or behavior pattern. Self-coaching helps you to recognize issues when a goal doesn't seem to fit or there is a dissonance between what you want and what you do. You can grow if you are open to considering your underlying motivation. In other words, why are you doing what you are doing, what are you getting or will you get out of it, and why it is important to you? Thinking the underlying "why" will require you to see quite differently about issues and goals. As you play with the why, you will discover new ideas and views about who you are and what you want.

PLAY WORK

- Listen as you tap into your inner coach and hear your internal greatness, business skills and external resources. What did you hear?

- Describe your greatest success out loud to yourself. List the greatness that allowed you to achieve your success.

- Listen with your heart rather than your head.

- Listen as you tap into your inner coach and hear your internal greatness, business skills and external resources. What did you hear?

- Describe your greatest success out loud to yourself. List the greatness that allowed you to achieve your success.

(continue to next page)

> ✓ Listen with your heart rather than your head.
>
> ✓ Listen with your heart rather than your head.

CHANGE YOUR VIEWPOINT

Many people, especially if they have never examined their lives in any way, tend to think of life from the bottom of the mountain. To change the viewpoint, you will need to go to the top of the mountain and look at the entire landscape of your life. Then think about what will make you happy and fulfilled, where you want to be five or ten years from now, what you want your legacy to be and what will give you peace, what your vision is, etc. You need to think in wonderfully broad terms about what you want out of your whole life, not just the present moment.

Changing the viewpoint can be an exhilarating process. However, you must be ready to climb to the top of the mountain and look fully at your life. When you are that ready, a very fast paced growth will occur and you should be prepared to hang on for the ride. It may not be a slow-paced train but a sky-rocketing one!

PLAY WORK

✓ Be fully present when you self-coach.

✓ Be practicing deeply listening to your inner coach and apply your tuning in skills to your inner conversations.

(continue to next page)

Coaching is for Everyone

- ✓ Give up wanting a self-coaching formula.
- ✓ Acquire a great sense of your language.
- ✓ Give up a need to be great at self-coaching and just self-coach.
- ✓ Be courageous: if a powerful question you ask yourself makes you uncomfortable, you probably need to ask it.
- ✓ Be willing to be wrong.
- ✓ Be willing to let the questions you ask yourself land.
- ✓ Have complete and total trust in your ability to handle the question and the answer.
- ✓ Come from your heart and never judge yourself.

Achieving Your Goals

Some self-confronting questions: "Where do I want to be at any given time?" "How am I going to get there?" "What do I have to do to get myself from where I am to where I want to be?"... "What's the first step I have to take to get moving?"

– George A. Ford

"Achieving Your Goals" is about the practical steps you need to take in order to go from where you are to where you want to be. In short, it is all about setting goals and then planning how to make those goals happen.

"Plan ... the moment you complete this, you will have given concrete form to the intangible desire." These lines by H. Stanley Judd say it all. Desires are but dreams. Having a goal and then a plan on how to achieve those goals provides the practical way that you can achieve your dreams. Planning your goals and then working on them may seem easy. You might even be wondering why this is a part of a book on self-coaching. Think, however, about the goals you have made. How often have you neglected to take even the first step toward making that goal happen? Or perhaps you got half-way through the process and stopped because something didn't work—you felt stymied or you lost momentum. Does this sound and feel familiar? Often a person is unable to work toward a goal, both major and minor ones, because

they do not have a plan and the support necessary to execute the steps necessary to achieve that goal. If you're nodding your head because you've been in that situation, be excited because right now you are going to learn the steps you need to take to achieve what you want in your life and work!

Self-coaching skills assist in developing a plan to achieve your goals and to provide the ongoing support, encouragement, and structure needed to complete the plan. You will not only learn how to develop the plan for a particular goal but also study other planning techniques that will give you a number of different self-coaching skills that will help you to design a strategy for achieving your goals. Because planning and doing, by nature, is an active process, this chapter requires much more activity than previous chapters. After all, a journey is never without action!

A CHANGE OF PACE

My approach to this chapter is to make the process of planning your goals very, very personal. You, I am sure, have a goal; maybe, it is to build a new career or to incorporate these self-coaching skills you've been learning into work you currently have, or maybe you are enjoying using self-coaching skills so much that you want to become a professional coach and sign up for coach training at www.CoachInstitute.com. Or maybe your goal is to simply become a better human being and have a better life with improved health and happy relationships. What I want you to do right now is to choose one goal to work on so that you can design your plan to achieve it.

Because I want you to actively plan out one of your goals, this chapter's directions are a bit more specific than the others. In order to make this process work well for you, I want you to read through the chapter up until the point that I tell you to stop. As you read, just read the play work, don't actually do it. The reason for this is that at the back of the book, there is an appendix that contains everything that you will find in the play work in this chapter. Appendix I is a Goal Planner Workbook that you can use to create your plan to achieve your most important goal. But, before you can really do the work that I want you to do in The Goal Planner Workbook, you need to understand the process. As you read this chapter and the play work sections, think about what the play work is asking you to do. That will make the process easier for you when you actually get to the appendix. **Creating a plan to achieve your goals is fun and rewarding. Take your time and learn the elements first.**

DEVELOPING YOUR PLAN

The reason why many people don't achieve their goals is because they don't have the right kind of plan to help them do it. Any good plan for achieving your goals will contain the following elements: a statement describing and defining what your goal is, an outline of the steps necessary to achieve your goal, an inventory of the resources necessary to achieve your goal, what resources are currently available, and recourses must be added. In addition a good plan includes a timeline for achieving your goal and must identify the individual steps along the way. A good plan also contains a structure to sustain momentum if the plan takes place over a period of time and ways to measure if progress is being made.

Throughout the planning process you need to ask yourself "self-confronting" questions and make appropriate observations so that you can develop the elements listed above. Above all, you need to be able to critically evaluate whether the proposed plan will achieve your goal, what challenges will be met along the way, and what commitment you have to make to execute the plan.

PLAY WORK

- ✓ Write down the goal you want to achieve.

- ✓ What is the reason you want to achieve this goal?

- ✓ How would your life change if you achieved your goal?

- ✓ How would you be happier if you achieved your goal?

- ✓ What steps do you need to take to make your goal a reality?

- ✓ List five to ten most important things you have to do to achieve your goal.

- ✓ Then number them in order of importance.

(Do not worry if you do not know all of these things yet. Remember, you're just reading this. When you go to the appendix, then you'll have a change to write them down.)

EXECUTING THE PLAN

Once you have developed your plan, the task of executing the plan begins. This is where you actually begin to take action and will begin to get excited and see forward momentum. With the support and structure provided by self-coaching skills, you will be able to look for areas where you are facing difficulty performing interim steps, maintaining momentum, staying focused, etc. When you feel stuck, you then evaluate and change the plan. If something is not working, check your personal commitment. Are you really committed to achieving this goal? Also, make sure that you maintain your momentum when challenges are encountered or progress is not as fast as expected. While it is important to put a time-line to your goal, it is more important to know that the time-line is there to keep you moving. You can change it if you need to, but having exact dates written down helps keep you on track and accountable. Most important, coach yourself to continually recommit to working toward your goal.

PLAY WORK

- ✓ What is the deadline that you will achieve your goal by?
- ✓ Take the five to ten steps you wrote down and put a date of completion next to each one.
- ✓ In order to achieve your goal do you have the time to achieve your goal? If not how will you create it?
- ✓ Do you have the energy to achieve your goal? If not how will you create it?
- ✓ Do you have the emotion and motivation you need? And if not, how will you create it.
- ✓ Do you have the money you need to achieve your goal? If not how will you fund your goal?
- ✓ What other resources will help you achieve your goal? How will you create those resources and put them at your disposal?
- ✓ When will you measure your progress and what progress will you expect for each date you do your measurements?

As you go through this process you will at times be joyful, sometimes frustrated, sometimes dejected. Self-coaching skills are the supports that lead you on; they are the even keels that remind you of the progress you made while assisting you to meet a current challenge in executing the plan.

Coaching is for Everyone

To help you understand this process more fully, I'm going to give you my goal planner for this book. As you read, you'll recognize all the questions listed in the play work.

1. The goal I want to achieve is: *Find a publisher who believes in my book and its importance like I do.*

2. The reason I want to achieve this goal is: *I have a burning desire to write a book that will help people have a better life, and I know I hold the secret tools they need.*

3. My life would change in the following manner if I achieved my goal: *I will feel like I am connecting with more people on the planet and making a contribution to them and that would bring me joy. Some of those people will also resonate with becoming coaches, and I'll be able to help them build the career of their dreams. I will also have more money to find my foundation and be able to do more good in the world.*

4. I would be happier if I achieved my goal because: *I would be living my life mission and at the same time fund my RSD foundation.*

The answers to the above questions have made me realize that I am truly willing to commit the time, energy, emotions, and resources necessary to achieve my goal:

Yes !!!!!!!!!!!!!!!!!!!!!!!!!!!!!!

I am now committed to my goal and ready to determine what I have to do in order to achieve my goal. There are several steps I must take to make my goal a reality. The five to ten most important things I have to do to achieve my goal are: (There are two steps to this process. First, write down all the steps you need to take. Do not worry about order when you're first writing them. After you get all the steps down that you need, then you go through and order them. This is why the following list looks like it's out of order. I did the list first, and then I ordered them.)

8. *Write the book*

1. *Ask my network who they know that can connect me with publishing contacts*

5. *Develop relationships with those publishers*

2. *Review the publisher's websites*

4. *Find someone, preferably live, with whom I can speak at those publishers*

3. *Develop my pitch*

6. *Give my pitch*

7. *Get agreement on them publishing my book*

9. *Edit the book*

I am committed to achieve my goal no later than *September 1, 2007.*

In order to do that I have to complete the steps I listed on the previous page by the times indicated below (re-list your steps from the prior page in sequential order and indicate when each can be realistically completed):

STEP DESCRIPTION	TIME COMPLETED
Ask my network for publishing contacts	*May 1, 2007*
Review the publisher's websites	*May 31, 2007*
Develop my pitch	*June 7, 2007*

Coaching is for Everyone

Find someone live I can speak to at those publishers   *June 15, 2007*

Develop relationships with those publishers   *June 30, 2007*

Give my pitch   *July 10, 2007*

Gets agreement on them publishing my book   *July 30, 2007*

Write the book   *September 30, 2007*

Edit the book   *October 15, 2007*

In order to achieve my goal and the interim steps toward it, I will need to have a variety of resources. I know I will need to commit time, energy, and emotion to the goal. There may be other resources I need such as money, technical help from someone other than myself or support from those around me to name a few. In this section, I am going to identify the resources I need, where they will come from, and if I don't currently have the resource, how I will get it. This will give me a blueprint for marshalling the resources I need to achieve my goal.

Resource No. 1: Time

In order to achieve my goal, I need __*10*__ hours per week. I currently have that time available. *Yes*

Resource No 2: Energy

In order to achieve my goal, I need energy to work on the goal. I currently have that energy available. *Yes*

Resource No 3: Emotion

In order to achieve my goal, I need emotion and motivation to work on the goal. I currently have that emotion and motivation available. *Yes*

Resource No 4: Supportive Network

In order to achieve my goal, I need a supportive network. I currently do not have this resource available. If I do not have it available, I can get it or create it. Below, I have listed how I am going to create the resource, where I am going to find the resource, and what steps I have to take to put the resource at my disposal:

I am going to explain to my husband I may need to work late at night to write. I am going to explain to my team that on certain days I will devote just to my book. I need to explain to my clients I may not return emails as quickly as I usually do because I am writing.

I want to be sure that, once I start working on my plan, I know that I am moving closer to achieving my goal. In order to do that, I would like to be able to measure my progress along the way. Below I have listed the times when I will stop and measure my progress. I have also listed what must have occurred by that time in order for me to know that I am moving closer to achieving my goal. I will use these measurements to correct my course, inspire me, and keep me moving forward until my goal is achieved.

Date of Measurement: *July 30, 2007*

Description of Progress That Will Have Occurred: *I will have found a publisher and come to an agreement at least verbally.*

Date of Measurement: *September 30, 2007*

Description of Progress That Will Have Occurred: *I will have completed the writing of my book.*

So dear friend, now that you have seen how I set up a goal, I want you to now turn to the Appendix #1, The Goal Planner Workbook, and I want you to go through each step and plan your goal.

Coaching is for Everyone

Welcome Back!

Now that you have taken your first steps to truly planning out your goals, I want to touch on three different variations of the goal planning process. These variations occur when you need to achieve a goal quickly, have one goal that you want or need to focus on, or when the goal or the plan needs to be significantly changed.

THE ACCELERATED PLAN

The accelerated plan is generally used when you want to achieve a goal quickly. Often, the goal is related to a business issue such as job change, increasing cash flow, or increasing sales. There is usually a feeling of immediate need to accomplish the goal or you risk some negative consequence. The accelerated plan always requires a greater commitment of time and energy and for that you have to enlist the support of those around you. To make this variation work, you must be fully committed to your goal and well motivated to make it happen.

Like the basic planning process, the accelerated plan has certain elemental steps. The first step is to commit yourself to achieve your goal quickly. Be sure you clearly identify your reason for wanting a quick result. Then, you need to come up with a meaningful time frame for achieving your goal. You will need to identify the amount of time and effort necessary to achieve the result within the desired time frame and then make both the time and effort available. Then you identify specific, interim goals and specific, interim measures to know if the plan is working and also identify whose support is needed and enlist that support. And then, of course, you must begin executing the plan. You must also quickly recognize any parts of the plan which are not working and what lessons are to be learned from those failures.

Executing an accelerated plan can be very demanding. To practice this, go back through your list of steps that you wrote down for your plan in the

Goal Planner Workbook. Identify which ones need to be put on an accelerated plan. Once you have the items identified, do the following play work.

PLAY WORK

✓ What are your specific, interim goals and specific, interim measures to know if your plan is working?

✓ What support do you need and how will you enlist that support?

✓ Who will you be accountable to while you are executing your plan?

✓ Begin executing your plan!

THE FOCUSED PLAN

The focused plan contains many steps similar to the accelerated plan, but the underlying rationale and emotion are dissimilar. The focused plan is used when you have several goals, but the achievement of one will cause the achievement of others to naturally occur. For example, you may want to make more money, have a bigger house, and drive a better car. The last two goals will naturally occur if the you make more money. Therefore, you must set aside the goals regarding the house and car and only focus on the goal to make more money.

The focused plan is also used when you have one goal that is much more important to you than any other goal. The emotions underlying the focused plan are usually different from the accelerated plan. While the accelerated plan commonly occurs in a "have to" situation, the focused plan reflects more desire than need. Therefore, your feeling of urgency is often less strong, and your potential consequence of failure less severe, and a longer time-line for achieving your goal is generally possible.

The key to the focused plan is precisely as the name implies: you must be focused on a single goal. To create and keep that focus, **choose a goal that will help you achieve other goals or that is of singular importance to you**. Know that you must commit to make that goal the focus of the plan and to temporarily set aside other goals. Develop a plan of action around that singular goal. Begin to execute the plan maintaining focus on the goal and, as always, measure progress at pre-determined intervals.

The focused plan requires a certain amount of persistence and patience. You should maintain focus, keep the goal fully in sight, make adjustments along the way, and remain accountable to the goal and at the same time remain easy and light-hearted throughout the process. With a light heart, now turn to your plan. If you were to focus on one and only part of your plan, what would it be and how would you do it? Evaluate your progress to date on your plan and achieving your coaching goal.

PLAY WORK

- ✓ Why are you committed to achieving your goal quickly?

- ✓ What is the reason you want a quick result and meaningful time frame for achieving your goal?

- ✓ What amount of time and effort is necessary to achieve the result you want within the desired time frame?

- ✓ Will you make both the time and effort available?

- ✓ Are you willing to focus on your plan and temporarily set aside other goals?

(continue to next page)

- ✓ Develop your plan of action around that singular goal.
- ✓ Begin to execute the plan maintaining focus on your goal.
- ✓ Measure your progress at pre-determined intervals.

CHANGING THE PLAN

Few plans, even the most thoughtful, are flawless because once execution of the plan starts, the learning process also begins. Particular steps may not have the desired result or produce the right progress. Anticipated resources may disappear, requiring adjustments. Your goal may change slightly or substantially, requiring an equal change in the plan. Once you begin to work on the plan, you have to become an astute observer to learn whether your plan or goal needs to be changed. Be sure to make observations like **noting when progress does not occur or does not occur at the pace originally plotted on the plan timeline**. You should analyze why progress has not occurred and make appropriate adjustments in your goal or the plan. Also note while progress is occurring. However, when the process becomes stressful, investigate the cause of the stress and come up with solutions to eliminate the stress. When you feel dejected or less committed, recommitment yourself immediately and investigate why commitment is gone, and what adjustments have to be made to restore commitment. Sometimes you might find that the goal is simply the wrong goal. Whatever the case, always be alert if a necessary resource disappears. Determine whether the resource can be replaced and if so, how. If it can't, what is the impact on your plan? And be willing to abandon your goal if necessary or if no progress is being made. However, if you choose this option, be sure abandonment is a conscious, purposeful and a reasoned decision by you.

Coaching is for Everyone

In addition to being a keen observer of how well your plan is working, you need to remove the concept of failure. Also, always be willing to identify the lesson learned if things are going well and really look at how the plan can be adjusted based on what you learned from your mistake.

The following play work isn't one that you're necessarily going to do just yet. However, I'm giving it to you so that you know it is there. It is really a check list that you can use when if and when things get tough and you need to change your plan.

PLAY WORK

- ✓ Note when progress does not occur or does not occur at the pace originally plotted on your plan timeline. Make appropriate adjustments in the goal or your plan to achieve the goal.

- ✓ If you feel stressed while making progress come up with solutions to eliminate the stress.

- ✓ Tune in and notice if you have lost your commitment. Ask yourself why your commitment is gone and what adjustments have to be made for you to restore commitment or if the goal is simply the wrong goal.

- ✓ Tune in immediately if a necessary resource disappears. Determine if the resource can be replaced and if so, how? If the resources are not or cannot be replaced, what is the impact on the plan?

(continue to next page)

✓ Be willing to let yourself abandon the goal if necessary or if no progress is being made. Be sure abandonment is conscious, purposeful, and a reasoned decision you are making.

Coaching is for Everyone

Truth

Truth is not beautiful, neither is it ugly.
Why should it be either?
Truth is truth.

— Owen C. Middleton

Throughout our journey you have heard me mention truth. Right now I am about to take you deep into the concept of truth. I am going to ask you to inhabit the world of seeking and being truthful. In this world, you will find that truth can take many forms and is different for different people. This world is both magical and powerful. In order to be in it, you must be open, present, and willing to be truthful.

Truth ties right to our previous section on goals. You need to know if what you have set as your goals are really things you truly want and you also need to assess whether your plan is in fact a plan that you can truthfully live up to. It is not important to set goals to please me or anyone else. Your goals must ring true for you.

"Whenever you have truth, it must be given with love or the message and the messenger will be rejected."

— Mahatma Gandhi

Coaching is for Everyone

You first heard about truth in "Tuning In." This chapter will be an expansion of those original concepts which taught you that you had an inner truth that your inner coach held for you. Here, you will study two different types of truth. You will learn about what I call "the truth" which is objective and identifiable, and second, you will also learn more about tuning into your own truth. Each of these types of truth has a key role in your life. Self-coaching skills help you to tell, hear, discover, and absorb these types of truth safely and without fear. Knowing the truth, you will be able to create that space and the power and magic that is required to achieve what you desire. Along with that power and magic, at the end of this chapter you will also notice that you will be more comfortable hearing and telling the truth, have begun to put a greater value on having truth in your life, have become more attune to what others believe is the truth, and will readily attach value to that truth as well as your own.

For this chapter, it is critical that you are willing to immerse yourself in the concepts I'm teaching you. The changes you will notice in yourself may be, at times, uncomfortable. Please stay with the material even if you feel somewhat ill at ease. Many of us have been taught to believe that what we think is always "the truth." It can be difficult at times to discern what is true for you, what is true for others, and what is factual truth. But, if you really take the lessons of this chapter to heart, by the end, you will have added a potent tool to your life.

YOUR COMMITMENT

I would like you to stop and think right now about what your definition is of the word "truth." How do you view it, and how do you use it? I want you to write your definition of truth and how you view it and use it here now:

_____

_____

_____

_____

_____

_____

_____

_____

_____

_____

_____

_____

_____

_____

_____

_____

_____

_____

_____

_____

_____

_____

_____

At the end of this chapter I will give you space again to notice what changes have occurred in the way you view and use truth. Please do not rewrite your definition until you have come to the end of this chapter...no short cuts please!

In addition, I am going to ask you to commit to telling your truth in a non-judgmental, non-charged way. On a daily basis, keep asking yourself if you've kept this commitment and if not, to identify what blocks stand in your way.

"THE TRUTH"

I often hear people use the term, "the truth." Almost as often, however, what the speaker is referring to is what the speaker has defined as his or her own truth. I also like the term "the truth," but it has a very limited meaning. "The truth" can be defined as those facts which are objective and quantifiable. Such facts might include the profit and loss of a business which can be mathematically calculated, the day an event occurred on (like birthday is December 29), or a historical fact that is not subject to dispute. The key is that there can be no debate about the fact I am calling "the truth" because it is indisputable. It does not reflect judgment, emotion, or interpretation of its existence or its effect. It simply is.

"The truth," quantifiable and objective, can often be confused with the impact of a fact, with the emotion you attach to a fact, or with the judgment you make based on a fact. Part of your core self-coaching competencies is to identify the objective truth and be able to tell the difference between facts and their interpretation. Once you recognize the objective truth, you can begin to make decisions on fact rather than assumption. This allows you to view your goals far more clearly and to plan to achieve those goals far more effectively.

There are a number of skills that you have already learned that will help you to recognize the objective truth. There are more powerful questions, observations, and related actions that will assist you to actually calculate or identify the truth for yourself, and I would like you to start identifying objective truth for yourself.

Your goal is to separate objective truth from your assumptions. To do this, you will have to affirmatively ask yourself whenever you think you know "the truth," and whether you are talking about an objective fact or your interpretation of a fact. If you are talking about your interpretation of a fact, please come back to the objective fact and label and identify it as such. See how your own view of the truth changes with this exercisePlay -Work

1. Think of an experience you have had and what you believe to be true about that experience. (For example: I recently had the experience of meeting a friend for lunch and learning more about cleansing. What I hold true is: I enjoy cleansing. I have done 7 cleanses. Cleansing helps me loose weight. When I cleansed I got my sense of smell back. My friend has done many cleanses. We both enjoy cleanses)

2. Now speak out load. What is YOUR truth, what is the other person's truth and what is THE truth? (For example): **My truth:** I have cleansed. I enjoy cleansing. I enjoy speaking to my friend about cleansing. I loose weight when I cleanse. I have done 7 cleanses. My friend does a lot of cleansing, too. We had lunch together and I enjoyed being with her and am grateful to have her in my life. **Her truth:** We met for lunch. We talked about cleansing some and about our health and husband's more. Terri cleanses as much as I do! Lunch went fast. **THE truth:** Terri has cleansed 7 times. Terri and Marlene met for lunch. Terri lost 25 pounds cleansing in September, 2007 for 20 days and she only drank water, lemon and cayenne pepper. Everyday she flushed by drinking 32 oz. of warm water with 2 T Celtic sea salt. They met at Arnolds Café for lunch. Terri got there 5 minutes before Marlene and picked out nuts and fruits she wanted. Marlene entered and they hugged. They sat down at a table. Terri got up and got menus. She brought them to the table. A waitress told them the specials. They asked for a few minutes. They ordered lunch. Terri got a protein smoothie, mushroom soup and a raw, veggie "BLT". Marlene got carrot juice and added a beat to it. They asked the waitress for water. She asked if they wanted ice and then said they didn't have ice. She brought them each a glass of water. They talked. The wait-

ress brought them napkins and silverware and food. They ate lunch. Marlene tasted Terri's soup. Terri had left over soup and took it home. Terri used the rest room and while she was doing that Marlene paid for lunch. Terri saw Maya who she hadn't seen for years and they talked. Maya's daughter ran out of the store and Marlene ran after her and carried her back in. Terri paid for her nuts and fruits and it cost $76.21. She used her Visa. She signed the receipt. She put a yellow copy of the receipt in her grocery bag. The waitress/cook wrapped her soup with plastic wrap and placed it in a cup holder with one napkin and one plastic spoon. Terri got a phone call from her editor that this book was done. They talked. Marlene used the rest room. Marlene and Terri carried Terri's packages to Terri's car. It was raining. Marlene had an umbrella and carried the umbrella and held it up for Terri. She also carried some of Terri's foods to Terri's car. Terri opened the trunk of the car and the car with her remote. The trunk opened up. Terri's car is green. It is a convertible. It is a Jaguar. It had yellow dirt on the left side. The foods were placed by Terri into her trunk. They hugged and said goodbye.

3. Can you see that YOU have a point of view and you saw an event through your own lenses and from your own shoes?

4. Notice that your truth and your friend's might be different. Accept your friend's truth as perfect and true for them.

5. Notice THE truth.

6. Can you see how much data and factual information was left out?

7. Now can you understand that what you believe, notice, value, experience is simply your observation based on your be-

liefs and values… the other person might not share the same feelings, beliefs, values, etc. and they are perfect and you are perfect in what you both believe.

8. However, THE truth IS the real data and is factual and isn't based on values or beliefs.

As you do the following Play Work, use this experience as an example. THE truth: Terri has cleansed 7 times. Terri and Marlene met for lunch. Terri lost 25 pounds cleansing in September, 2007 for 20 days and she only drank water, lemon and cayenne pepper. Everyday she flushed by drinking 32 oz. of warm water with 2 T Celtic sea salt. They met at Arnolds Café for lunch. Terri got there 5 minutes before Marlene and picked out nuts and fruits she wanted. Marlene entered and they hugged. They sat down at a table. Terri got up and got menus. She brought them to the table. A waitress told them the specials. They asked for a few minutes. They ordered lunch. Terri got a protein smoothie, mushroom soup and a raw, veggie "BLT". Marlene got carrot juice and added a beat to it. They asked the waitress for water. She asked if they wanted ice and then said they didn't have ice. She brought them each a glass of water. They talked. The waitress brought napkins and silverware and food. They ate lunch. Marlene tasted Terri's soup. Terri had left over soup and took it home. Terri used the rest room and while she was doing that Marlene paid for lunch. Terri saw Maya who she hadn't seen for years and they talked. Maya's daughter ran out of the store and Marlene ran after her and carried her back in. Terri paid for her nuts and fruits and it cost $76.21. She used her Visa. She signed the receipt. She put a yellow copy of the receipt in her grocery bag. The waitress/cook wrapped her soup with plastic wrap and placed it in a cup holder with one napkin and one plastic spoon. Terri got a phone call from her editor that this book was done. They talked. Marlene used the rest room. Marlene and Terri carried Terri's packages to Terri's car. It was raining. Marlene had an umbrella and carried the umbrella and held it up for Terri. She also carried some of Terri's

Coaching is for Everyone

foods to Terri's car. Terri opened the trunk of the car and the car with her remote. The trunk opened up. Terri's car is green. It is a convertible. It is a Jaguar. It had yellow dirt on the left side. The foods were placed by Terri into her trunk. They hugged and said goodbye.

PLAY WORK

- ✓ Think of an experience you have had and what you believe to be true about that experience. (For example: I recently had the experience of meeting a friend for lunch and learning more about cleansing. What I hold true is: I enjoy cleansing. I have done 7 cleanses. Cleansing helps me loose weight. When I cleansed I got my sense of smell back. My friend has done many cleanses. We both enjoy cleanses)

- ✓ Now speak out load. What is YOUR truth, what is the other person's truth and what is THE truth? (For example: My truth: I have cleansed. I enjoy cleansing. I enjoy speaking to my friend about cleansing. I loose weight when I cleanse. I have done 7 cleanses. My friend does a lot of cleansing, too. We had lunch together and I enjoyed being with her and am grateful to have her in my life. Her truth: We met for lunch. We talked about cleansing some and about our health and husband's more. Terri cleanses as much as I do! Lunch went fast.)

- ✓ Can you see that YOU have a point of view and you saw an event through your own lenses and from your own shoes?

- ✓ Notice that your truth and your friend's might be different. Accept your friend's truth as perfect and true for them.

- ✓ Notice THE truth.

(continue to next page)

- ✓ Can you see how much data and factual information was left out?

- ✓ Now can you understand that what you believe, notice, value, experience is simply your observation based on your beliefs and values... the other person might not share the same feelings, beliefs, values, etc. and they are perfect and you are perfect in what you both believe.

- ✓ However, THE truth IS the real data and is factual and isn't based on values or beliefs.

YOUR PERSONAL TRUTH

"Your personal truth" is simply what you believe is true. Your truth may include not only objective truth, but also feelings, opinions, values, judgments, and assumptions. It is your view of the truth and that view imprints how you see, hear, and feel situations and decisions. One of my personal truths, for example, is that people are basically good.

Your truth can include past, present, or future. That means that you can carry experiences and patterns from the past that impact present decisions. You could be responding to present impressions or senses, or be relating present actions to future consequences. Thus, your own truth is not only a belief; it is also how that belief impacts you.

Self-coaching skills help you to separate your truth from "the truth" as well as help to identify the components of your truth. When looking at truths, it is also essential that you be willing to acknowledge if the truth is preventing you from moving forward. To illustrate, here is an example. You may say **"I have money problems."** This statement is your truth that you do not currently have enough money. This, however, is only the start of the exploration. From this statement, you have to discover: "the truth." What is the money problem quantified? Rather than simply a problem, what is the actual number size of the problem? What are the cause and the result of the problem? What is the truth about how it is impacting the rest of your life? What is your view of how the problem can be solved? What is your truth about preventing the problem from reoccurring?

At the end of an exploration like the one I just gave you, your truth might be the same or it may be completely different. At the conclusion of the above example, you might decide your truth to be **"I don't have enough money to pay my bills, and I must get a second job,"** or **"I actually have more than I thought,"**, or **"I've decided not to judge myself by the fact I don't have enough money."** So through self-questioning, analyzing, and experimenting with your truth, you will take the value from the truth and use it to move forward. And as you are already aware of, self-coaching skills assist you in looking at behaviors, patterns, or situations in a different way and help you to use that new view as a means to take a new direction to move forward.

Again, mastering the art of looking at your truth non-judgmentally and without attachment is an incredibly powerful self-coaching skill. To hone this skill, I am going to ask you to notice your own conversations on a daily basis. When do you present your truth as the truth? When do you raise your truth as more important than the truth of others?

Once you have recognized your truth, practice presenting and identifying it as your truth with an opening for others to tell their truth as well. What have you noticed as you practice? Finally, as I mentioned at the beginning, I would like you to consider your original definition of truth now that you have come to the end of this chapter. If there are significant changes in the way you view truth now, please rewrite your definition and compare it. Have you gained enlightenment? Have you realized the truth?

PLAY WORK

- ✓ Now redefine your truth without looking back to the start of the chapter.

_____

_____

_____

_____

_____

_____

_____

_____

_____

_____

_____

_____

_____

_____

_____

_____

_____

_____

- ✓ With what you have learned now how do you define truth, why it is important to you, and how do you use truth?

Coaching is for Everyone

Play

*And young and old come forth to
play on a sunshine holiday.*

– John Milton

Oh enlightened one. I am calling you enlightened as you now have gained the knowledge about truth from the previous chapter! But now, how about having some fun? Surprised and confused? Well you are going to study play as a self-coaching skill. In the last chapter you got focused on the distinctions between the various truths. Often we are so caught up in our beliefs or truths and making ourselves right that we take ourselves, or work and our lives, way too seriously. So now it is time for you to learn about play. And because this chapter is about play, this chapter requires you to play and play with gusto. Let's start by setting the tone and the mood.

Please close your eyes and imagine yourself as a child again. See yourself playing with friends and siblings. See yourself on the playground, in the sandbox, baking mud pies, or hitting a baseball for the first time. Feel the freedom and the laughter. In this world, you have no adult cares, just the pure happiness of childhood. As you inhabit this world, think now of the three activities that you did as a child that gave you the greatest sense of joy. Feel that joy and freedom again and with that in your mind, open your eyes. Do you have your joy still with you? Good. Now you have the space and emotion you will need to keep as you read this chapter.

Coaching is for Everyone

If you now feel your adult side returning slowly, it is probably asking "what this is all about and why is play called a self-coaching skill?'" To answer se questions, please think for a moment about how you felt as you returned to your childhood and let go of adult cares. I have used the words freedom and joy quite purposely in describing that place, and I am sure that while you were there, you felt freedom and joy as well as a certain lightness of being.

As adults, we tend to lose our sense of experimentation, imagination, adventure, freedom, and joy. As a result, we feel heavy and weighed down. Often, we are unable to picture a life of joy because you have not felt that pure childhood sensation for a long, long time and in fact, wonder if it is still possible.

In coaching, I have found that if you learn to recapture the openness and lightness of childhood, you begin to become freer and more creative about who you are and where you are going. You actually begin to look for the work and activities that bring you joy rather than weigh you down. Once you have recaptured play, you be will willing and able to play harder and more exuberantly with your life. As a result, you will grow and move forward at a much faster pace than the adult who is weighed down.

"Without this play… no creative work has ever yet come to birth.

The debt we owe to play of the imagination is incalculable."

– Carl Jung

You will see this change in yourself as you play in this chapter. The change is important. Therefore, you must recapture your ability to play, experiment, imagine, and be adventurous. That is, in part, what this chapter is all about. Finally, as you may have noticed, play is about activity rather than text, spontaneity rather than thinking, so you will have playful assignments rather than text to read. The use of play as a self-coaching skill will come from your assignments rather than from me telling you what play is about and how to use it.

With that said, I ask that your only two commitments relating to this chapter are to actually participate by playing and by being open to see the power and effect of play. Now let's head to the playground!

PLAY WORK

Returning To Childhood

- ✓ Spend an hour at a park or playground simply watching children play. Join in if you want. See what happens as you watch, and if you decide to join in and play, see what happens as you play.

- ✓ Go to a toy store and buy 2 to 5 toys that really appeal to you. They can be things as uncomplicated as bubbles and a wand or something that requires somewhat more skill to do. The only criterion is that the toys must be something you want to play with and do not require you to think like an adult. Once you have bought the toys, your assignment is to play with them.

- ✓ Go to a bookstore and pick up a great children's book to read. Anything from "Horton Hatches an Egg" to "Charlotte's Web" to "Winnie the Pooh." Read your book and notice where it takes you. If you have the opportunity, share the book with a child along the way by reading aloud.

(continue to next page)

✓ Choose one of the three childhood activities that gave you joy that you remembered when you closed your eyes earlier. Do that activity.

Using Your Imagination

✓ Create something fun out of your imagination. Use crayons, paints, paper or any other medium. You can draw, write, color, create a model—you choose. The only requirements are that the project be easily doable and that it is incredibly fun.

✓ Grab two friends and have a round robin story contest. One person starts and talks for two or three minutes; the next person continues, and so one. Please make the story light and fanciful, something like a tall tale or a fairy tale or an adventure story. No adults as the central character please!

✓ Purchase a no words story book (the "Big Dog Carl" books are good ones) and tell the story out loud to someone, preferably a child.

✓ Go to the zoo or the park and make up a story about the children or animals as you watch or walk.

✓ Choose one playful thing of your own that will ask you to use your imagination. Please be as silly or as playful as possible.

LOSING CONTROL

Children are marvelous at using spontaneity and adventure to create their world. Adults have instituted relatively significant controls on both these characteristics. The assignments below are about absolute freedom to "be" rather than the rules we place on ourselves. By the way, I am asking you to lose control, not be at risk. So choose fun activities but not any that would put you in physical danger. Sky diving and bungee jumping are not required to lose control!

This is another area where you might feel uncomfortable at first. When you feel that, try thinking about being wonderfully adventurous instead and then, of course, go play!

PLAY WORK

- ✓ Think through what one fun activity would make you feel completely ridiculous. Go do it.
- ✓ Think through what activities would make you feel just a little not in control. Choose one and do it.
- ✓ Call one or two friends and tell them you want to do something completely spontaneous. See what you think up and go do it.

You have now spent great time playing! I want you to now answer the following questions to integrate what you have learned and to do whatever you put as the answer to the last question.

PLAY WORK

- ✓ As a result of playing, what have you discovered about yourself that you had forgotten?

(continue to next page)

Coaching is for Everyone

- As a result of playing, what new strengths have you discovered about yourself?

- As of result of playing, what new possibilities do you see?

- As a result of playing, how have you become lighter?

- Now that you have played, what is the funniest, most playful "homework" you can give yourself?

Change

It is not the strongest of the species that survive, nor the most intelligent, but the one who is most responsive to change.

– Charles Darwin

Change is an essential part of life. You probably decided to learn self-coaching skills because you want to change something. Sometimes, the changes you are looking for are quite large, ranging from career to lifestyle. Other times, the changes are the slight nuances that give your life its sense of small pleasures and easy moments. Whatever the change sought, you never learned self-coaching skills and find you either have not been or cannot be successful in implementing the change on your own.

In this chapter you will learn about the types of changes you will seek, the stages of the change cycle, the challenges of change, and specific areas where you can make the changes you seek. So at the end of this chapter, you will not only be more comfortable with the idea of change but also welcome changes as a wonderful part of life for you. You will also gather knowledge necessary to create forward movement in the change process and understand different types of change. As Stephen Covey said: **"People can't live with change if there's not a changeless core inside of them. The key to the ability to change is a changeless sense of who you are, what you are about, and what you value."**

Coaching is for Everyone

Because I would like you to integrate this material into your life right now, please identifyidentify one change you would like to make. Keep that change in mind as you read through this chapter.

THE NATURE OF CHANGE

In this section, I am going to talk about the nature of change. You will be given a broad overview of the types of changes that you may encounter and this discussion of change will further inform you about challenges that occur during change.

Before I start with the steps you need to take to change, it is necessary to understand what change is about. While each change is described separately, please remember that any change will often contain two or three of the characteristics below. You should be able to identify the characteristics presented by the changes that you want. Know what is best for you based on the change characteristics combined with the knowledge you have of yourself.

As you go through the next few pages, think about yourself and any transitions or changes you are going through. How would you categorize your changes? If you identified the type of change, how would you think differently about what you are experiencing?

Changes can be categorized in a number of ways. I categorize change by the degree of change occurring and the underlying motivation driving the change. The easiest area to describe is what motivates change, so I'll start off there.

WHAT MOTIVATES CHANGE?

Change is generally motivated for three reasons. Change is **reaction-ary** when it is in response to something that has already occurred. You have been fired or you are in debt, or you have made others angry, or you have been told that you don't manage well, or maybe you have been diagnosed with a chronic illness. These are all examples of situations that will cause you to react by looking to change. For me, I had a reactionary change when I found out I had RSD.

Change is **anticipatory** when it is undertaken in anticipation of something that will occur in your future. Examples of anticipatory changes include when you know that your industry will be downsizing, when you begin to plan for life after your current career, or when you see a significant life shift on the horizon and want to plan for it. I personally experienced anticipatory change many years ago when I knew the company my husband was working for was going bankrupt.

Sometimes you cannot identify what you want to make different or change. There is simply an **unknown feeling** that not all is well or that somehow things could be better. This is no less a motivator for change than reaction or anticipation even though, at the beginning, the identification of the specific reason for change is more vague. This was me at forty. I knew there was more in life and I needed to do something different with my life but I couldn't identify what.

From a self-coaching perspective, it is important to identify your driving motivation behind your change. Is change meant to correct a current problem or have a long-term effect? Is it to deal with a work situation or create more personal happiness? The motivation will have a significant impact on your change strategy and the measurement of your change results. So, two of the first questions to ask you as you contemplate change are **"Why do you want to make this change?"** and **"How will you and your life be better if this change occurs?"** Such questions will allow you to understand the underlying motivation and goal driving your desire to make the change.

Coaching is for Everyone

TYPES OF CHANGE

Along with having different motivations, change can also impact different areas of your life. The two major areas of shift are personal and professional change. Within those two areas, though, are clearly discernible sub areas. **Foundational change** occurs when you seek to change something personal that is fundamental to 'who you are'. Consequently, the change is profound and deep and requires significant effort to make. Examples of foundational changes can include extreme simplification of your life, substituting collaboration for control, or giving up your attachment to money. A foundational change only occurs when your view of life will be fundamentally different when the change is complete. I made a big shift in my foundation when I stopped identifying myself through my job title.

Revelatory change occurs when you allow some hidden characteristic that is truly part of you to come to light. In other words, revelatory change occurs when you step into your true self in all of its manifestations. When you decide not to be perfect, allow your whimsical side to become public, or express your hidden competitiveness freely, then you have made a revelatory change. Revelatory change occurs when your public and private persona become exact matches. I know that when I became a coach, I started acting more freely. I was more my fun self, and I made revelatory change in my life.

Habitual change is exactly as it sounds. It occurs when you change a habit that does not serve you. Habitual change occurs when you either let go of a habit or replace an energy draining habit with a habit that serves you in a positive way.

Yes indeed my big one was letting go of cigarettes when I was in my twenties. Later, a smaller one was letting go of hanging around with negative people, thinking I could make them feel better.

Foundational, revelatory or habitual change can occur both in your personal and professional side of your life. The changes may be incremental, that is, a simple tuning or slight redirection, or acute, involving a complete transformation or profound adaptation. Again identifying the type of change will allow you to determine your strategy, the amount of time the change may take, and the challenges that may occur along the way.

Now that you know some of the types and degrees of change, can you identify what type and degree of change you need and as a result, determine how much commitment and effort you will need to effect the change?

THE CHANGE PROCESS AND ITS CHALLENGES

The change or transition process has a number of key steps to it. Sometimes, the steps happen in sequence. At other times, some of the steps happen simultaneously or in a different order than that listed below. Each step, however, is an integral part of change if the change has any depth to it and few transitions feel complete unless the steps have occurred.

One of the steps is the **recognition that change is occurring**. This means that you realize that you are in the middle of change (particularly true if change is reactionary) or about to start change. You begin to assess the size of the change and usually feel somewhat uncomfortable that change must or will occur.

Another step is **factual disengagement from the past**. Here you begin to intellectually let go of the current state and accept that a new state or situation must or will be occurring.

Emotional disengagement from the past is another change step. As your intellectual engagement becomes stronger, your emotional disengagement follows. Often, emotional disengagement is more confusing and turbulent for you, even though intellectually you recognize the need for and benefit from change. You may feel confused, disoriented, and sad. These emotions are normal during the change process and usually vary with the deepness of the change. The more profound is the change, the greater your emotions.

Another phase of change is **identifying the change that is occurring and the anticipated end result of the change**. During this phase, you identify both factually and emotionally what is occurring and what the result at the end of the process will be. A portion of this process is articulating the end goal of change. The other component is identifying the practical steps that must be accomplished for change to actually occur. For example, you might identify changing careers as the end goal. The interim steps identified might include identifying values, tying those values to your self expression through work, researching types of jobs or careers, choosing a career to express your self–values, adding additional skills, and the actual job hunt process. As you can see, identifying the change, its steps, and its ultimate resolution gives you a certain reality and practicality to your change process.

Few changes occur exactly as planned and all require learning new lessons or new habits of some kind. Expect a **learning curve**. A new job may need new skills, a new pattern of communication may mean giving up your habit of being right, a new lifestyle may mean giving up your old toys and the perception of yourself self through those toys. Because learning is generally not instantaneous, it requires recognition of what is being learned and repetition to internalize the lesson. Such recognition and repetition takes time. That period of time is the change learning curve. During this period, you will need the assistance of your self-coaching skills to clarify the lessons and take the appropriate actions to internalize them. The learning curve is also the place where you can get discouraged during change.

Let's discuss the step of **internalizing the lessons and applying them**. At this juncture, you are inhaling all that you have learned and using the lessons to take significant actions towards your end goal. Because you are doing this, the change process intensifies both in quality and quantity. When this happens, just know that the goal is within reach, and the change will shortly be complete.

Now let's look at when **change and transition are complete**. At some point, you know that you have worked through to the end of your goal and are willing to declare yourself done with the particular change and its accompanying transitions. You have fully and completely said good-bye to the past and have embraced the future that you have created for yourself. The work and lessons of change are embraced and integrated. It is time to rest and acknowledge the work.

The change process can be easy or turbulent, peaceful or a struggle. Self-coaching skills can ease the turbulence by educating you about the change process and helping you to find where you are in the process at any given moment. Intellect, hard work, combined with good self-coaching and patience will help you move to the next step and ultimately complete the change process by achieving your goal.

As Steven Covey's quote indicated at the beginning, those who deal best with change are those who have a clear sense and understanding of their personal core. You need to know yourself on the whole, complete, and not subject to change. It is that part of the personal core that will sustain and aid you through the change process. In addition, you need to know what part of your life is constant and will provide stability both internally and externally during change and also provide a base to return to throughout the change cycle. Along with knowing your personal core, you should also have a sense of your greatness and strengths to use as tools. This knowledge will help you to deal far more easily with change.

Further, you should form and implement small steps immediately for achieving interim goals as change often takes place over a period of time, and it needs not only a jump start at the beginning but a revitalization in the middle. You should develop small goals within the larger change goal, so there are positive wins throughout the change process. This allows momentum to build and be sustained over time.

Coaching is for Everyone

Every person in change needs cheerleaders, people who believe in them and their goals. Build a support team made up of people who care about you, who will help you, and encourage you throughout the change process. This will exponentially assist you with meeting the change cycle from a position of power and strength. And every change victory should be celebrated to give you motion and momentum to the next step.

However, change never occurs without a stop or stall somewhere along the way. Immediately recognize when your progress has stopped and either adjust your plan or take extraordinary action to recharge the change process.

Sometimes, change is so blocked that you must go completely "out of the box" to un-stick yourself and the process. These moments require extraordinary, highly unusual, and very bold actions. This takes courage, patience and "losing control" or to go just a little crazy in order to move forward.

Lastly, you should know when change will be complete and what evidence is necessary for to recognize that change is complete. Revisit both topics on several occasions through the change process. This will give you a sense that the change goal is actually achievable and when it can be achieved.

The above challenging areas are the most common in the change cycle. As you work through change, use the following play work to guide you through the process.

PLAY WORK

- ✓ How can you be more comfortable with change as a wonderful part of your life?

- ✓ What changes are you committed to making over the next four weeks?

(continue to next page)

- Identify and define the major change you will make.

- What is the result you want from this change?

- What part of your central personal core will keep intact during this change? (For example, if you change your job you are still "you".)

- Remind yourself of your greatness.

- What are the critical themes you need to change in your life? (example, greater peace, more calm, less stress, working less)

- What change strategy and structure can you use that reflects your greatness and strength?

- What are some small steps you can implement immediately for achieving your interim goals?

- Who can support you during your change?

- How will you celebrate motion and momentum at each step of change?

- How can you recognize when change stalls?

- How will you create the time, opportunity and method to say goodbye to the old?

- How can you recognize when change stalls?

- How will you create the time, opportunity and method to say goodbye to the old?

- How ill you lose control when necessary?

- How will you define when change is complete for you?

Coaching is for Everyone

Simplicity, Balance, Rules, and Limits

The ability to simplify means to eliminate the unnecessary so that the necessary may speak.

– Hans Hoffman

These next two chapters will deal directly with personal issues that occur frequently as you go through the change process. To create your life that is truly perfect, you need the ability to resolve these issues with the help of the necessary self-coaching skills.

This first personal issues chapter contains four topics: Having a simple life, creating balance, formulating rules for your life, and establishing limits on what you will do or permit. As you think about these four topics, what do you think the theme is? One easy way to look for the theme is ask yourself, **"What would be different or what would I get, if my life were simple? What if I felt in balance, I had rules by which I lived my life, and I established limits on what I would do or permit?"**

Often, you believe that because a certain area of your life does not appear perfect, it is "wrong" or something needs to be "fixed." That is not true; your life is not wrong, you are not deficient, or in need of fixing. All you need is to discover, to change for the better, and to grow!

Coaching is for Everyone

"I will grow. I will become something new and grand, but no grander than I am now. Just as the sky will be different in a few hours, its present perfection and completeness is not deficient. So I am presently perfect and not deficient because I will be different tomorrow. I will grow and I am not deficient."

– Wayne Dyer

This brilliant piece of wisdom from Wayne Dyer reflects the truth of life. "Now" is perfect, but we can make it more meaningful, interesting and worthy of living. You are ready to change, explore, and discover where your life can reflect who you are in a deeper way. As you embark on the adventure of personal growth in your life, remember that you are whole, complete, and perfect as you start and as you grow.

HAVING A SIMPLE LIFE

Leading a simple life enables you to keep what you think is necessary and throw away whatever is not needed. When you can clean your cluttered life, you can then define priorities and live by your own rules. Simplicity brings discipline and a zeal for future development.

As Wayne Dyer says, having a simple life allows you to easily distinguish between what is necessary and what is not. In contrast, a complicated, cluttered life creates a state of confusion where the driving force is trying to "keep it all straight" rather than creating a life that is easy and joyful to live.

KNOWING IF YOU HAVE A SIMPLE LIFE NOW

In order to determine whether having a simple life is an appropriate issue for you to apply your self-coaching skills, you must first look for clues. If you find yourself saying you never have time and always feel behind; or you do little or nothing to take care of yourself; oryou talk about being disorganized; or you mention messy or cluttered environments frequently; or you are unable to devote time to your goals, then you aren't living a simple life. When you feel that you present a picture of overwhelm, lack of time, and disorganization, then you may need to create a simpler, more elegant, more workable life. In fact, often simplicity is not only desirable, it is necessary to create the time, energy, space, and money to achieve your true goals. You must "clear the plate" in order for a new conviction to be created.

When I became a coach my life was far from simple! My house was cluttered and I constantly was searching for things I had misplaced. I felt frantic and was always running from thing to thing and place to place.

THE STEPS TO HAVING A SIMPLE LIFE

Once you recognize that your prosperity lies in a simpler life, you must introduce the concept of having a simple life and proceed with the relevant changes. This involves a few important points. First, identify a goal or issue that you already have an interest in pursuing; second, relate that goal or issue to having a simple life; third and last, identify how having a simple life would help achieve your goal or handle the issue.

These three steps allow you to recognize and take ownership about abouthaving a simple life. You can begin exploring what a simple life will do for you, and when you do that, you create a more uncomplicated world of your own. But all the same how do you recognize whether your life needs this concept? Well to begin with, you need to first pay attention to eight critical areas that will help you ascertain your requirement of a simple life.

Coaching is for Everyone

Start by identifying areas of your life that are complex and are consuming time, money, emotion, or energy. Also identify what you would get or have if the complex areas were simpler, easier to manage, and less consumptive for you and identify why having a simpler life would be meaningful for you. Look at significant, impact areas to simplify and for each area that you want to simplify, develop a plan to simplify that area of life permanently. For each area that you want to simplify, identify immediate actions so that you can begin simplifying and make present progress. Identify what kind of support and participation is needed from others in order to simplify each area of your life and also identify the rewards that are occurring and what you are discovering about yourself as your life becomes much simpler.

I began with simplifying my home. I hired an organizational expert to help me organize my kitchen, closets and garage. I got rid of old clothes had less clutter and could find my pots and pans easier and knew just what was in my pantry. My office had fewer books and a lot less paper. It was quick and easy to find the information I was seeking and also simple to get dressed into clothes I knew fit and looked great on me.

Now that you know much more about how and why to have a simple life, it's time you choose one area of your life to simplify. Go through the steps listed in the following play work and determine your responses to each step. You can take little steps or big steps, you can take the stairs or the elevator, the aim is to reach the goal. Then spend the next few days doing things that will simplify the area of your life you chose to work on.

PLAY WORK

- ✓ Identify areas of your life that are complex and are consuming your time, money, emotion or energy.

(continue to next page)

✓ Identify what you would get or have if the complex areas were simpler, easier to manage, and less consumptive for you.

✓ Why would having a simpler life be meaningful for you?

✓ Identify significant areas to simplify, areas that impact your life.

✓ What are easy areas for you to simplify?

✓ For each area you want to simplify develop a plan to simplify that area permanently.

✓ For each area you want to simplify identify immediate actions you can take to begin simplifying so that you will make progress.

✓ Identify what kind of support and participation you need from others in order to simplify each area of your life.

✓ Move into action by making a powerful request of yourself.

✓ Identify the rewards that will occur and what you will discover about yourself as your life become much simpler.

CREATING BALANCE

Balance: the word has a lovely feel and sound to it. We often hear people talk about creating a balanced life. Rarely, though, is balanced defined. What is balance? Webster's Dictionary defines balance as "equipoise between contrasting, opposing, or interacting elements," "bring into emotional and mental steadiness," and "bringing into harmony." These definitions are remarkably applicable to the people who have achieved balance in life. When you have created balance, you have equipoise between contrasting, opposing, and interacting elements of your life. You have brought your

Coaching is for Everyone

life into harmony and have found an emotional and mental steadiness that serves you well.

Probably, the amount of "balance" in your life varies widely. Because balance is lacking or may be at a low level, your life may be driven by attempts to juggle all that is happening around you, by the sheer need to catch up and keep up, or by reaction to whatever the most pressing item of the moment is. Hence, it is at this juncture that self-coaching introduces you the concept of creating balance.

Let me first share my personal story with you. My life was 90% career focus. I worked, I traveled for work and took planes everywhere and was in airports much of the time.. When I was home I was thinking about work, preparing for work, checking email, voice mail or getting paged about work. Work ran me. I was exhausted and had little free time with my family and friends and even when I did I never fully shut off my work mind. My life was unbalanced. I was in poor health with constant colds and the flu, I was tired and run down and overweight. I didn't eat right or get enough sleep and made no time to work out. Community involvement and spiritual practices were missing from my life. I was like a flat tire! My life was definitely out of balance.

KNOWING IF YOU ARE OUT OF BALANCE

Many of the clues relating to a need to have a simple life also reflect a need to create balance. You have to identify a few things such as: Does your lifestyle reflect an area or areas that dominate your life at a high cost to you? Do you seem short on time and long on stress and seem to "juggle" life, reacting to whatever is most prominent in any given moment? Further, do you at all reflect any sense of equilibrium and calm, and if so, how much? Do you have a choice or are you simply responding to what you believe is important? Does your mind reflect peace and happiness or "have to," "ought to," and "should" drivers?   Do you have free time or have you scheduled yourself so that your calendar is always full and are you always busy? Is your ability to respond to yourself and others is based on lack of time rather than quality of life and service?

Whew!! And that's not all. Do you feel that you need to be right, make people happy, or seem to think that every task must be completed personally by you? Can you let go at any time and recognize a need to slow down? Last and foremost, do you feel the need of more balance in your life? If you see any of the above signs, and particularly if you see many of these patterns, an introduction to the concept of balance may be in order.

HOW TO CREATE BALANCE

Introducing the concept of creating balance is much like introducing the concept of having a simple life. If, after reading the above, you realized that your life is out of balance, I can guide you on how and when to introduce this concept into your life.

The first things to identify are the patterns of stress overwhelm, lack of time, etc. that inhabit your life. Then you need to identify, generally, the costs associated with lack of balance and further define what would be different if you created more balance. Creating balance is probably slightly more challenging than having a simple life. Creating balance generally means that you will have to change the way you live and the choices that you make. This will sometimes feel big and uncomfortable, and at times, you will resist moving forward. You must, therefore, be quite clear about what you feel. Are you ready to choose to change? Are you ready for the balancing act? Start figuring out when and how to balance your life by going through the following play work. Ask, understand, and identify, and let your intuition and the guidance rendered by these skills tell you which step is appropriate and when.

PLAY WORK

Answer these questions fully and honestly.

- ✓ Do you feel out of balance?
- ✓ Define where you are or feel out of balance.
- ✓ Define what balance would look like, feel like, and how your life would be better if balance where present and please state truthfully if you want balance and are willing to commit to getting it.

You need to understand that balance is about treating yourself as important and valuable and to understand that balance means that you will have to make choices and say NO to things, demands, and people, and that holding yourself first for a while is okay.

So, identify what's important to you and what's filling time or filling an identified need and then begin to make choices based on what's important to you, what will honor who you are, and to begin to say no to other things. Begin with small steps if necessary or large steps if possible, but continue to "clear the plate" until you feel balanced. Stop along the way if you need and want adjustment time. At some point, you will probably have to make what feels like a very large choice. Be clear, firm and decisive. Understand that balance is a continuum and you are working towards the perfect spot on the continuum.

Creating balance can take time, so a lot of patience that is required! Moreover, throughout the process, personal growth has to remain constant. Now it's your turn to work on balance so please consider where and how you want your life more balanced and why. Go through the steps and determine your responses to each step. Then spend some time in actions which will create more balance in your life and give due weight to your personal growth!

FORMULATING YOUR RULES FOR LIFE

Formulating rules to govern your life and your personal behavior, and setting limits on what you will do and permit, are the key elements in having an easy, clear, decision-making process that will allow you to have a simple life and maintain balance. I have found, almost without exception, that people who do not have rules and limits lead complicated, fragmented lives. Their lives seem, at times, to be run by all the things they have agreed to do, all the tasks they don't want to do, and their reaction to people and situations that upset them. Often, these people want clarity. However, clarity will not arrive until they have regained control of their life and time.

SEEING YOUR GAPS ION RULES AND LIMITS

There are four major clues to look out for, clues that depict your need to establish rules and limits. Do you seem to be doing much for others and little for yourself? Do you have substantially more activities than you can handle? Do you feel overwhelmed and never have down time? Are you often unable to complete your own important work due to the press of other commitments and time taken up by others? Do you have an inability to say "no" when requested to do things and feel the impact of others on your life to such an extent that you react to the way you are treated by others?

I had many problems in these areas. I said "yes" to all social events and to requests to help friends or family even if that put me more out of balance. I was in a constant state of overwhelm and felt frustrated all the time. In addition I let people at work walk all over me. Ihelped them with their projects and their work and then had to work extra hours all the time just to keep up with my own work. I had few rules and limits and this added to my general feeling that life was way too hard and too much of a struggle.

When there is incongruence between what you want to do and what you are actually doing take the hint that it is time for you to concentrate on setting rules and limits. The basic question that I can ask you is—**Do you seem to struggle with deciding what's most important or how you should be spending your time?** If yes, then you need to establish some structures that would make it easier for you to decide and help you simplify your life. The concept of rules and limits disciplines your life, gives you a sense of direction and helps to take only those decisions that reflect your values and not feel conflicted or restricted.

INTRODUCING RULES TO YOUR LIFE

When I refer to rules for your life, I am talking about setting rules that govern your own behavior. When you have rules, you have established principles that will guide your conduct. Rules include basics like **"I will not tell lies,"** or **"I will treat others in a mannerly, respectful way."** Rules, however, can go further. The more specific a rule is, the more it simplifies your decision making process. For example, you may extend your rules to include **"I will live my life according to my values."** Once you have established such a rule and have identified your values, then you can easily decide what to allow in your life. If a task or person would not reflect your values, that task or person does not enter your life. The decision is simple because all you have to do is apply the rule to come to a conclusion.

As you can see, rules serve as instant decision makers and often as instant eliminators. If you have rules that truly reflect who you are, you will also have a life that reflects who you are. As with simplicity and balance, 'to start setting rules' has steps that can occur in a variety of orders. Establishing rules is often a gradual process to start but once started you naturally begin to establish rules for yourself and begin to see results. And once you do this, you will begin to feel lighter as rules help create a simpler, more meaningful decision making process.

To begin to start setting rules you will first identify where setting a rule would make your life easier. Then, identify how this area of your life would change and be more like what you wanted if you set a rule that worked. I recommend you start by setting one or two rules that you believe will simplify the way you deal with a particular type of situation, decisions, etc. The rule can be big or small, depending on what you are ready for. When you set your rule, you can either make it permanent if you are sure of the rule's potential effectiveness, or you can "try the rule on" for a week and see what impact the rule has. Be sure to think whether you will have any challenges honoring the rule. If so, create a structure to support yourself. Always check back, and if you feel that the rule has improved your life, go for the next rule. Also, think about whether there should be modifications to the rule to make it work better.

Remember, if you cannot agree on how to rule yourself, someone else will rule you. So beware—your life, your values, and your future growth are all in your hands. But my little sermon is over, and now it's your turn to create a rule that will simplify your decision making.

PLAY WORK

- ✓ Choose one rule to install and know what you want as a result of having the rule.

- ✓ Then, devise a way to make the rule a part of your life. See what you learn.

ESTABLISHING LIMITS

Setting rules is setting standards for yourself. Establishing limits is setting standards for how others must treat you and/or interact with you. It is often easy to set rules for yourself. It is far more challenging to establish limits that others have to adhere to. Establishing limits, however, is crucial to having a balanced life. People without limits spend their time giving control and energy away to others instead of using it for themselves. For example, do you spend time complaining about how you are treated by others? That time spent complaining is control and energy that you are giving away to the very person you are complaining about. Think about yourself. How much time and energy do you give away to others in relation to activities or behaviors that you do not like? By establishing limits and keeping those limits intact returns control and energy to you.

HOW TO KNOW IF YOU NEED LIMITS

When you feel continually bogged down by issues involving others, disturbed and ill treated, or that often others dominate your time, you probably need to learn about establishing and keeping strong limits. The tell tale signs that you may need to establish limits are the same as for formulating rules for life. Here they are again: Do you seem to be doing much for others and little for yourself? Do you have substantially more activities than you can handle? Do you feel overwhelmed and never have down time? Are you often unable to complete your own important work due to the press of other commitments and time taken up by others? Do you have an inability to say "no" when requested to do things and feel the impact of others on your life to such an extent that you react to the way you are treated by others?

INTRODUCING LIMITS IN YOUR LIFE

When I refer to establishing limits, I am talking about setting limits about how others must behave around you. Examples of limits include **"You cannot raise your voice to me,,"** or **"You must use respectful words around me,"** or **"You cannot lie to me and still be my friend,"** or **"You must contribute to nurturing our relationship in order to be part of my life."** When you establish and maintain limits, you install a system that protects you from costly people and behaviors. As you continue to augment your limits and enforce them more, you will find that tasks, people, and behaviors that have a negative impact and consequence will naturally disappear from your life.

To establish limits you need to decide what behaviors or activities by others are going to be eliminated from your life. Determine what limit will eliminate the behavior or activity and set the limit. Communicate the limit to the appropriate person at an appropriate time and ask that the limit be respected. Above all, enforce the limit if necessary. Establishing and keeping limits requires you to inform others what your limits are. Then, you need to either request specific behaviors or request the cessation of specific behaviors. This process will generally make you feel somewhat at risk and uncomfortable, particularly if you have not established limits in the past. Therefore, you need to be prepared to put this new idea into practice and stop spending a lot of time and energy in doing things you don't want to do.

As with previous topics, establishing limits has some steps which can occur in a variety of orders. With limits, however, it is particularly important that you identify what the end result of establishing the limit is. With that knowledge, you can maintain the motivation and strength necessary to announce a new limit, request that it be honored, and enforce it if necessary. To establish and keep limits, first identify where establishing a limit would eliminate an energy drain, create less struggle, and/or make you life and decisions easier. If you have difficulty identifying where to establish limits, think about where you expend negative or wasted energy or what you consistently complain about. Ask yourself: if you established a limit that worked, would an area of your life or a relationship change and be more like what you wanted?

Start with one or two limits that you believe will simplify the way you deal with a particular type of situation, person, decisions, etc. The limit can be big or small, depending on what you are ready for. Adopt the limit and you can make the limit permanent if you are that sure of the limit's potential effectiveness, or you can "try the limit on" for a week and see what impact the limit has. Communicate the limit to appropriate people and to ask that the limit be honored by those people. Decide what actions you will take if the limit is not honored. Think whether you will have any challenges honoring and keeping the limit. If so, create support structure to assist in communicating the limit, requesting that it be honored, and then have strategies and actions that will be taken if the limit is not honored. Check back and see how the limit worked. If you feel that the limit has improved your life, go for the next limit. Also, think about whether there should be modifications to the limit to make it work better.

Like setting rules, establishing limits is often a gradual process to start. In addition, since establishing limits means making requests to others, the process is usually difficult at first but once you are determined enough and consistent in following the steps, you are rewarded and feel complete. So what are you waiting for? Establish limits that stop energy draining activity in your life and begin to see how much easier your life is when meaningful limits are established and kept.

PLAY WORK

✓ Where would setting a rule or limit make your life and decisions easier?

(continue to next page)

- ✓ How, if you set a rule or limit that worked would this area of your life change and be more like what you wanted?

- ✓ Come up with one or two rules and one or two limits that you believe will simplify the way you deal with a particular type of situation or person. The rules and limits can be big or small depending on what you are ready for.

- ✓ Try on the rules and limits for a week and then you can decide to keep them or let them go depending on the impact it has for you.

- ✓ What structure or extra support might you need in honoring the rules and limits you just set?

CONQUERING YOUR FEARS

"To conquer fear is the beginning of wisdom."

– Bertrand Russell

It is sometimes said that fear is life's biggest motivator. Most often, however, fear as a motivator goes unspoken and unrecognized. Instead, you believe you are acting out of a sense of right, a sense of accomplishment, or a sense of provision. When the layers are peeled away, however, fear of something or fear of not having something turns out to be what is guiding your behaviors.

Coaching is for Everyone

Just to demonstrate, take a piece of paper and write down quickly, without thinking, your four largest fears. Write what intuitively pops into your mind. Now, take that list and really think about how many of your actions over the last month were taken to address those fears. Are you surprised? Don't be. It is a human condition to have fears and work to meet the hunger or need those fears represent. For you, however, fears need not be the driving forces in life.

"Where fear is, happiness, peace, and wisdom are not."

– Seneca

These words reflect the core of this chapter—the self-coaching skills you need for identifying and overcoming your fears. The information given here will help you to identify your fears, help you to see the truth about them, and act to eliminate them in four areas: money, truth, leftovers, and self-belief. In doing so, you will gain a better life. You will discover the confidence to lead, and also you will learn how to use fear as a motivator. I would like you to work on your own fears in one or more of these four areas just listed as you go through the chapter. This will not only make you practice these self-coaching skills but also help you gain a better and improved way of living. Therefore, be ready to banish fear and replace it with wisdom, peace, and happiness.

ELIMINATING YOUR FEARS ABOUT MONEY

In our society, money and fear around money is regularly a common motivator. From defining yourself by what you have to incurring substantial credit card debt, money is a significant factor in your everyday life. Because as a society we are a world overly concerned with money, money is frequently given a substantial amount of your personal energy. Statistics tell us, for example, that attitudes and behaviors toward money are the most frequent cause of marital strife. Money is also the topic that most people feel most uncomfortable talking about. Moreover, studies show that people often stay in jobs they dislike because "the money is too good." In short, people often let money drive them instead of using it as a tool for happiness. This behavior is based in fear: fear that there won't be enough money; fear that without certain accoutrements a person won't appear successful; fear of the future, or fear of behaviors around money from the past. Thus, your relationship with money will determine much of your behavior and your level, or lack thereof, of peace and happiness.

The telltale signs regarding money issues are quite easy to spot. If you have this fear you will talk about credit card or other debt, you will have on-going discussions with others about money, you will worry about how much is in the bank, or you will talk about the last new toy you purchased. Money and financial state are, however, simply facts. The emotion, worry, and energy around money are completely and fully invented by you, just like all worries and all emotions. Don't forget you are in charge of your emotional attitude and because you are in charge of your emotional attitude toward money, that attitude can be changed if you wish. In short, you can, with your own work, be wholly in control of your relationship with your money just like all areas of your life.

And now that you are aware about the hold that money has over you, how about putting that knowledge to practice?

PLAY WORK

I have provided an assessment that you can use to know more about your money issues in Appendix II at the back of the book.

(continue to next page)

Coaching is for Everyone

- ✓ Please make a copy and do the assessment for yourself.
- ✓ See how it feels and where it's difficult.

  Get pennywise and discover true happiness!

ELIMINATING LEFTOVERS

When you read this title, I bet you got an image. The image might be something cold and greasy that's been left in the refrigerator. You don't want to eat it, but at some point you have to take it out and look at it in order to decide to finally throw it away. Once it's thrown away, it no longer takes up room in the refrigerator and you no longer have to think about it every time you open the refrigerator door. While "leftovers" in a self-coaching context is not about food, the image discussed above does have similarities to the self-coaching definition.

A "leftover" is something that continues to occupy your thought in a negative way. You may only have a few leftovers or you may have lots of them. Some examples of leftovers include continuing to think about the way a person has treated you, dwelling on something you did in the past that you wish you hadn't, or continuing to put up with clutter around you. Leftovers have an effect. They take up your thought, emotion, energy, and like that dish in the refrigerator, space. Because they have not yet been thrown away, there is less room and space for positive growth and emotions.

There are generally two ways you can toss out leftovers. The first is to take some action that will make the leftover disappear. Using the examples above, those actions might include talking to the person that you believe mistreated you and bringing the issue to closure; apologizing for whatever happened in the past and forgiving yourself as well; or cleaning up the space around within the next week. Whatever the action, the goal is for you to remove the leftover completely from your life.

The second method allows you to change your attitude towards the leftover. This method is usually used when the situation that created the leftover cannot be changed. In order to change an attitude towards the leftover, you must recognize and label the leftover, recognize the leftover's current impact on your emotions, thoughts, and life, and then commit to reclaiming the power you have given to the leftover. In short, you can say: I can't change the leftover, but it won't control who I am, how I am, or how I react.

Self-coaching skills will help you identify what leftovers you have in your life, determine whether you want to get rid of them, determine what method is best to deal with the leftovers, and create a plan to "throw the leftovers out" once and for all.

Now that you have a definition of leftovers here is your play work.

PLAY WORK

✓ Your assignment is to identify three leftovers in your life.

✓ Now develop five ways you might approach each of the leftovers.

See the assessment for eliminating leftovers provided in Appendix III to help you with your own leftovers—to stock them or to discard them.

INVITING TRUTH IN

Once again our old friend truth has to be invited back in. A beautiful life can only be born of a beautiful and truthful mind and that my friend will tell what you exactly where you are and the authenticity of your dealings. Often one of our biggest leftovers is a missing truth. Perhaps you have told a little white lie or many of them. Perhaps you hide behind what you really want to say and don't voice your truth. We have to become truthful or we have leftovers that compromise our honesty and our real voice.

So, here we are, back to our old friend "truth." This time I am going to focus on truth in a different way. Here, I am going to focus on your truth and how to assist you with recognizing, honing, and using that truth in the most authentic way possible. I use the word "authentic" purposely. Often, out of fear, we disguise our authentic selves. We unwittingly, un-meaningfully, and occasionally with intention, change who we are or how we appear. We make changes to suit what we want the outside world to think of us. Consider yourself for a moment. Has there ever been a time when you made an excuse for being late that wasn't fully true or exaggerated an accomplishment to make it seem better than you thought it was? These are small examples of where you let your fear of how you are perceived, or how you might perceive yourself, dictate your actions. You hide your authenticity among all the ways you believe you should or could be, instead of simply being who you are. And after you compromise your authenticity, what happens next? Next, you worry that you will be found out. Someone might discover you're not perfect, that you aren't as good as you seem, or you might be called to account for that little excuse you made for being late.

Mark Twain once said that if you tell the truth, you never have to worry about what you said. It is equally accurate that if you are authentically yourself, you never have to worry about who you should be. The purpose of the self-coaching skills I am about to present is helping you be authentically yourself, without artful disguises, and willing to invite truth into your life.

There is a myriad of telltale signs that will tell you that you're not being authentic. Your conscience will tell you of how you are or might be perceived by others. You will notice incongruence between your words and your actions. You will find yourself striving to obtain things that will define success in an external way, but still not being happy or comfortable. This is a delicate but critical area. You have to recognize and name those areas where you suffer hidden costs from not inviting the truth in. Once you recognize the freedom of inviting the truth in you gain the confidence necessary to be fully authentic and to actually begin to tell the full truth all the time. Once you step into this realm, hidden costs will disappear and you will become much lighter very, very quickly. And that is when truth prevails and you get a clear picture about yourself and your life.

So in order to sharpen your vision, develop five clues that you might listen for in this area. In addition, think through and write down five costs that you have to bear when the truth is not invited in. In order to assist you, I have provided in the appendix an assessment about truth. Do the assessment in Appendix IV now and see what you learn about yourself in this area. And then come back and return to your play work. Bon Voyage!

Now with your leftovers complete and your ability to see your truth, it will be easy to do this activity.

PLAY WORK

- ✓ Write a story about your three greatest successes.

- ✓ Create a list of your ten greatest accomplishments and what you had to o to achieve them.

- ✓ List ten ways you have contributed to the lives of those around you in the last month.

- ✓ Keep a journal of the little things you do everyday that serve yourself and others.

(continue to next page)

- ✓ Describe your greatest success out loud to yourself. List the greatness that allowed you to achieve your success.

- ✓ Listen with your heart rather than your head.

- ✓ Listen with your heart rather than your head.

- ✓ Listen as you tap into your inner coach and hear your internal greatness, business skills and external resources. What did you hear?

- ✓ Describe your greatest success out loud to yourself. List the greatness that allowed you to achieve your success.

- ✓ Listen with your heart rather than your head.

Leading a Charmed Life

A happy person is not a person in a certain set of circumstances, but rather a person with a certain set of attitudes.

– Hugh Downs

J ust like the chapter entitled "Play," this personal issues chapter is about assisting you to bring lightness, humor, joy, and fun into your life. These characteristics, all rolled into one, may be characterized as content- ment. You may be wondering why I call it a charmed life. It is because it is a life that seems to have its own enchantment and magic. As you do more and more of the work from these chapters on personal issues, you will notice that parts of your life will be working much better. Your goals and desires will seem to come more quickly and easily. You will move through problems and challenges easily and without struggle. Your peace and happiness quotients will be high and your stress and worry quotients will become low. In short, your life will soon become wonderful.

I am guessing that you, like most people in general, wish to be happier and more at peace. You may have different problems and issues such as **"a need to change careers," "a wish to be a better manager"** or **"a want to be more organized."** What you really mean is, **"I want to feel more peace- ful," "I want to have burdens lifted from my shoulders,"** and **"I want to be completely happy."** In addition, I have noticed that there seems to

Coaching is for Everyone

be an important and real connection between your level of contentment with yourself and your life and your ability to achieve your stated goals.

"Nothing can bring you peace but yourself."

– Ralph Waldo Emerson

And how true! To date, every self-coaching skill you have learned is about helping yourself discover what you want, where you want to be, and how to get there. The advanced skills in this chapter will interweave with the skills you have previously read. These skills will give you a unique set of tools that will assist you to work at a deeper, more meaningful level on your personal fulfillment while you are also working on more "outside" goals such as changing careers. The personal coaching skills in this chapter are divided into four areas: peace, happiness, passion, and what I call "living a charmed life." In each area, you will find assessments, exercises, and even some games that you can use. These are meant to give you a base to relate with and I also hope and expect that you will develop better understanding and gain the positive attitude you so require.

SELF-COACHING SKILLS FOR PEACE

Webster's Dictionary defines peace as a state of quiet, tranquility, and freedom from disturbance. I am certain you would like a life that has an attitude of tranquility and freedom from disturbance. Life is not, generally, conducive to quiet and tranquility. Instead, in almost every aspect of life, overload and agitation seem to drive out peace. The externals of life seem to get busier and more complex leaving little room for serenity. Therefore, as my quotes at the beginning indicated, attaining quiet and tranquility must come from within yourself. It is developing a certain way of being with, looking at, and responding to your life. In addition, because external life is so busy, there is often very little feeling of peace. In fact, you must practice the feeling of peace in order to begin to develop a sense of what will give you tranquility and contentment.

When you constantly feel agitation or a state of turmoil, or when you want to create more "downtime," self-coaching around the concept of peace may be just the thing for you. On the next few pages, I have provided some advanced questions, exercises, and games that will assist you in learning about, experiencing, and creating peace. There are, by the way, some themes about peace which underlie the questions, exercises, and games that follow. See what themes you can discover.

PLAY WORK

Questions Related to Peace

- Would you like to have a more tranquil life?
- What would tranquility and peace feel like for you?
- How would a peaceful life look and be different than your life today?
- What is the most important attitude you need to change in order to be more peaceful?
- What are you willing to give up in order to have more peace?
- What do you do on a daily basis to bring peace into your life?
- What is the smallest thing you can do to add peace to your life?
- When are you most peaceful?

(continue to next page)

- ✓ Are you willing to set aside some time to practice being peaceful?

- ✓ If you were truly peaceful, how would your view of yourself change?

- ✓ Can you remember a time when you felt peaceful? Please describe that time and what you were doing.

- ✓ What would you do if you had no responsibilities?

- ✓ How do you currently practice peacefulness?

- ✓ Are you willing to be peaceful all the time?

- ✓ How would your relating with and to others change if you were incredibly peaceful?

Games

- ✓ The Peace Game: See how many times a day you can create peace for yourself and give yourself a really great reward each time you create that peace. Rewards can be reading your favorite book, eating what you like most or simply spending time the way you enjoy!

- ✓ Involving Your Family: Take the peace game to a new level by making it a family activity where everyone chooses their own reward. Another variation is to have your family, co-workers, and friends point out when you are not being peaceful and then be rewarded for doing so.

- ✓ Give Peace A Chance: Think about 3 to 5 things that make you peaceful. Then, do at least one of those things everyday and write three sensations you had while "giving peace a chance."

(continue to next page)

At the end of this game, you are sure to achieve better rewards that only you can identify for yourself and continue to build peace based on that learning.

- ✓ The Emotion/Habit Game: Most of us have a dominant emotion or habit that interferes with peace. It can be anger, annoyance, tolerating, complaining, etc. Identify the emotion or habit that is blocking your peace and develop a game to play that will "call" you to awareness when you get into the emotion or habit. If you can't come up with a game, use a variation of "The Peace Game" to get started. At the end of the game, identify what you learned about your own pattern and what you think the next step in the peace process is going to be for you.

Now, dear reader, you must be aware that the mind attains peace when it has solved its conflicting thoughts. So, as you travel across the realm of self-coaching, unravel yourself and attain calmness of mind. "Peace can not be kept by force. It can only be achieved by understanding." How truthfully and aptly do these words of Albert Einstein reflect the gist of this chapter!

SELF-COACHING SKILLS FOR SECURING HAPPINESS

You want to increase your level of happiness just like the rest of us. You want to start each day with a sense of joy at waking up and end each day with a quiet, contented feeling that the day was well spent. I am certain you want to feel emotions such as pleasure, delight, gladness, and gratitude. In order to work on creating more happiness, you have to create an environment that is light, fun, and vibrant. As you add more happiness to your life, you will notice a change in yourself, you become more free and easy, seek out and

Coaching is for Everyone

have more fun, become gentler, have better relationships with others, and above all feel a lot nicer towards yourself! Soon you will get accustomed to being truly happy; you will begin to set rules and establish limits that will protect your happiness, need less external validation, and will naturally eliminate things, people, and attitudes that interfere with staying happy.

Self-coaching skills will assist you to reach this place quite quickly, and they will dramatically increase your happiness and to play life as a big game in order to do so. In the following pages, I have again provided questions, exercises, and games to help you play large in this arena. Remember, as with the concept of peace, the questions, exercises, and games are just tools, not a formula for sure success; your success is determined by how diligently you use them.

PLAY WORK

Exercises for Happiness

- How are you already happy and what has created that for you?
- How much time of the day do you spend doing things that make you happy?
- On a daily basis, do you affirmatively choose to do things that will make you happy?
- Are you willing to give up unhappiness as an emotion in your life?
- What do you truly like about yourself?
- If you had to spend time doing only things that make you happy, what would you be doing? What wouldn't you be doing?

(continue to next page)

- If you only spent time with people that made you happy, who would that be? Who wouldn't you spend time with?
- What emotions do you need to add to your life to be happier?
- What emotions or attitudes would you have to let go of to be happier?
- What can you do for one half hour every day that would make you happy?
- How much fun do you want in your life? What are you willing to do to get it?
- How much of yourself do you express on a daily basis?
- If you were a master of happiness, how would you be different and how would your life be different?
- Do you have enough now, today, in your life to be fully and completely happy?
- Are you willing to have the intention to be happy?

Exercises for Gratitude

- Everyday, list ten things you are grateful for.
- Start each day by listing five things you deserve to have, then make at least three of them to happen.
- At the end of each day, make a brief list of things you did well and acknowledge your accomplishments.
- For one week, keep track of how many times a day you were happy and why.

(continue to next page)

✓ Try to double the number of times you are happy in the next week.

✓ Keep a happiness journal for the next 30 days.

✓ Commit to spending as much time as possible in the next week with people who make you happy. Make this an important priority in your life.

✓ Make a list of the top ten reasons you deserve to be happy.

Games for Happiness

✓ The Don't Do It/Be Happy Game: Tell those who love you that you intend to be happier. Give them a list of ten things that you do that makes you unhappy or that interfere with your ability to be happy. Every time they catch you doing one of those things, they get to "punish" you by choosing a happy thing that you must do.

✓ Don't Do It/Be Happy Game, Part II: See how many times you can say no to things and people that make you unhappy. Establish rewards for saying "no" 10, 25, and 50 times. Then, celebrate how much happier you are.

✓ The One Whole Day Game: Commit to being happy for one whole day and doing only those things that make you happy for that day. Have a friend or loved one play the game with you and see if the two of you can out do each other at happiness.

✓ The Pied Piper of Happiness Game: Your job is to be the pied piper of happiness for an entire week. You must be a model of happiness and lead others toward it by the magical way you

(continue to next page)

act while you are happy. Keep track of any happy magic this creates for you.

Your mind is like a garden, which may intelligently be cultivated to produce a rich harvest of happiness and like the saying goes…the secret of getting ahead is getting started, so dear friend, practice happiness as an everyday occurrence in your life and reap the riches of the ultimate bliss that comes from living a happy life.

SELF-COACHING SKILLS FOR INDUCING PASSION

In this personal issues chapter, you've been studying about living a charmed life. Passion is the last piece you will read about before we talk about how to identify a charmed life. Passion is one of those elusive qualities of life that you often want but don't know quite how to describe. When I talk of passion from a self-coaching perspective, I mean that you are doing things you love, value, and feel excited about in all aspects of your life. Like peace and happiness, the ability to get and keep passion in life is a process. You might make statements such as **"I want to do something I really love," "I want to put more meaning into my life,"** or **"I hate my job and I want to do something else."** In fact, what you may really mean is, **"I want my work and my life to reflect the things that are important to my heart, mind, and spirit"** and/or **"I want more passion in my life."**

When you feel the need for more passion, you need to determine if you are looking to align your life's activities (especially work) around the things that are important to your heart, mind, and spirit. Once you have discovered your passions, you can then more fully incorporate those passions into your life. However, if you do not know what having passion in life would look like and what that would mean (and most people don't), then your next step is to first discover your passion.

The questions, exercises, and games in this section will focus mostly on how to discover your passions. PPassion is about creating greater happiness, joy, energy, and lightness in life. Your attitude should reflect those characteristics in order to create a wonderful life where passion can make an appearance.

PLAY WORK

Questions about Passion

- ✓ Define what gets your juices flowing in a positive, energizing way.

- ✓ If you didn't have to work, what would you do?

- ✓ Name the five characteristics or things that are important to you that most define who you are. How can you reflect those things more in your life?

- ✓ If you looked at when you are most creative, what are you doing, how are you doing it, and why are you doing it?

- ✓ If you identified when you are most energized, what are you doing, how are you doing it, and why are you doing it?

- ✓ What's the secret thing you've always wanted to do, but never done?

- ✓ If you gave yourself permission to be completely childlike and do exactly what you wanted to do, what would it be?

- ✓ What are the things you do that are joyful and that you never procrastinate about?

(continue to next page)

- ✓ Complete this sentence: When I grow up, I want to _____.
- ✓ When things seem to come naturally and easily to you, what are you doing?
- ✓ What would people around you say matters most to you?
- ✓ What would people around you say you like to do most?
- ✓ If people around you defined when you are happiest, what would they say?

An Exercise To Create the Life You Desire and Deserve

- ✓ Imagine a clear canvas that is your life. Now draw your life on the canvas exactly the way you want. Know that it is a masterpiece. Do this over the next week adding a different section of the drawing every day in words or by actually drawing the picture. Be carefree and spontaneous while you do this. Put no limitations or pre-conceptions on what the picture will look like. Explore what you come up with.

- ✓ Make a list of the ten things that give you a natural high. Keep a log for a week noting every time you do one of those things. At the end of the week, look at how much time you spend with these things versus energy drainers and see if you have any conclusions or ideas as a result.

- ✓ You have five years and only five years to live. Create a plan for the next five years that will make your remaining five years truly fulfilling.

- ✓ Spend _____ (amount of time) everyday doing something you are completely and totally passionate about.

(continue to next page)

Games for Happiness

- ✓ The Adventure is My Passion Game: Sometimes passion can be discovered during an adventure. Choose one activity that is completely out of the ordinary for you. Give it a try and see what you learn about yourself.

- ✓ The Ferris Bueller Day Off Game: Choose a day and tell your family and friends that you are taking a day off from reality. Spend the entire day doing only things that are totally fun and totally passionate for you. What did you learn?

- ✓ The "But They Told Me To Do It" Game: Ask your family or best friend to choose three activities for you to do in the next 30 days that they think will appeal to your passionate side. Whatever they choose, you agree to do. See what you learn about yourself.

- ✓ The Pump Up The Passion Game: Choose one activity that really gives you pleasure and sense of yourself. Double the amount of that activity in your life over the next 30 days.

Finally, I must say that passion is the driving force that takes life forward, and in Alexander Pope's words **"On life's vast ocean diversely we sail, reason the card, but passion is the gale."** Discover, explore and delve into your personal core and find the pearl of passion. Happy diving!!

The end result of doing the play work in this chapter is you getting into this magical rhythm. After you have led a charmed life for a few weeks stop and recognize your own growth and changes and acknowledge your accomplishments. BBe sure to celebrate! Celebrate not only your achievements but that you will now lead a charmed life forever!

Leading a Charmed Life

As I have told you earlier, before I learned self-coaching skills my life was busy doing things I didn't even want to be doing. This ranged from my job to having friends I really didn't love to be around and to being polite and saying "yes" to every social invitation no matter how much inside I wanted to scream "no". I was surrounded by clutter in my home and had trouble thinking and getting organized. I constantly felt stressed and rarely laughed or fooled around. I had little free time and when I did have free time I spent it doing things I thought I "should be doing". Nothing came easy in my life and I was constantly ingpushing and everything I did required constant effort.

As I learned self-coaching skills my clutter began to disappear. My home became organized. I simplified everything from my clothing and cosmetics to my business. I I carefully selected fun, joyful friends. I learned to be less stressed and began to feel peaceful for the first time in my life. I laughed more, was silly more and allowed myself to be more child-like even when playing with my nieces and nephews and great nephew and niece. Life was more fun - actually I was more fun. I saw things more clearly and took all of life less seriously. My biggest gift was that I began to live in flow. I now live like the waves on the ocean rolling in and out and knowing all the chaos of life is simply the stuff life is made of. So I ride with it and I don't push against it. This sense of loving acceptance and connection with my inner coach also brought about my connection to spirit and knowing there is a higher universal force that I am part of. This energy of vibration creates the rhythm and magic in my life as I let things come to me easily trusting in the universal power and in myself.

Coaching is for Everyone

The World of Coaching

The greatest gift I can give to others is to coach them to find their passions and to live their lives with joy and delight in each moment!

— Terri Levine

I saw the power of coaching so many years ago when my own coach helped me to define who I was, to rekindle the "Terri" inside and to let go of the loss of my mother and my inner sadness. As I learned about myself and got honest about what I wanted, I quit my corporate job to align with a career that would allow me to assist more people to get in touch with their childlike authentic selves and to live without "shoulds" and "ought-tos". I had no idea when I hired my first coach that shortly after that I would be a life and business coach and would be working in this profession full-time, at home I literally found the career I was born for. I am fully aligned with who I am, and the work not only provides me income, it serves the planet as well.

It is magical for me to wake up each day and to coach people around the world who are serious about making changes to improve their lives, to work and to live with integrity, and to honor their values. I feel blessed that I can connect with the individuals and companies I coach and thank them for allowing me in their lives in this deep and trusting way.

It was a surprise in my first year of coaching that so many people started asking me to train them to use coaching skills in their lives and how many more would have the desire to coach others and to be committed to making a serious difference in people's lives. As my coach training school emerged, it did so to serve two audiences. The first audience is the masses who have never learned coaching skills and have so much desire to change their lives and be more fulfilled. The second audience is the business owner, entrepreneur or person who desires to have their own business and sees that coaching full- or part-time is right for them as a start up business or in addition to their current profession.

Every day I watch the graduates emerge from the coach training program at www.CoachInstitute.com and stand proud of how they are living from their hearts and playing full out and enjoying their lives and work with such gusto! It is inspiring to know that they are changing the lives of others every single day, too.

All coaching students learn self-coaching skills first. They know that to learn coaching, including self-coaching, takes practice. You are now finished reading *Coaching Is For Everyone*. You have all the tools you need to do self-coaching, but to get results you must practice all the skills I teach you in this book. Learn them by living them one at a time.

If you have a yearning to advance with them and you would like your own Certified Personal Coach Trainer SM to assist you, I am happy to provide you that connection and any additional resources you might need as a student of coaching skills. You may want to learn coaching to better your life or to advance your career. You may want to learn to be a self-coach simply for the sheer joy of it. Or you may want to practice these skills on others as a hobby, or you may wantto become a full time or part time life or business coach. If you do, visit www.CoachInstitute.com and discover the world of advanced coach training. That is an adventure that awaits you now that you finished this journey!

With your new found skills you can not only help yourself, but you can touch the lives around you with the attitudes you have developed. Keep practicing! Keep discovering! Keep working and exploring! Keep striving and keep growing! So, my wish for you is that, each day, you can enter into the pages of your life the same immortal words that Christopher Columbus wrote in the log of the *Pinta* as he faced danger, storms, hunger, mutiny, and fatigue in the uncharted Atlantic: **"This day we sailed on!"**

BON VOYAGE!

Coaching is for Everyone

A Note from Terri

I have a deep respect for coaching skills and passion to share them with others. I hope this book has expanding your mind and improved your life and I hope you'll suggest family, friends, and co-workers get a copy, too!

Are you a little curious about coaching as a career?

Do you want to know a little bit more about coaching?

Would you like a free audio report that goes along with this book?

Then go directly to:

www.COACHINGISFOREVERYONEBOOK.COM.

Finally, I say to YOU, start living right now with more zest and gusto, more joy and freedom. Honor yourself as the unique gem you are. Watch yourself sparkle and glow and be appreciative of yourself and others.

Your coaching skills have now trained you and energized you to start living full out! I dare you to be bold and live from a new place... the place of the authentic and beautiful YOU!

Finally, if you want to know about my products and services related to self improvement, please log on to: www.TerriLevine.com.

And if you would like to know about how you can have me speak to your organization or company, please visit www.TerriLevineSpeaks.com.

If you are curious what else I recommend to expand your learning, please go to www.TSentMe.com.

Thank you for the honor and privilege for allowing me to be your "coach" on this journey. I wish you all you desire and so much more!

Love,

"T"

Coaching is for Everyone

APPENDIX I

THE GOAL PLANNER

INTRODUCTION

This planner is designed to provide you with a step-by-step method to plan how to achieve your most important goals. It is easy to use and, when complete, should provide you with a road map to take you where you want to be. You will know what you want to achieve, how long it should take, what you need to get there, and how to measure your progress.

To use the planner, simply answer the questions on the next few pages. The questions are meant to cause you to think, so you may not have the answer immediately upon reading the question. That's okay. The more thoughtful you are in answering the questions, the more complete your plan will be.

Use the planner for only one goal at a time. If you have several goals, make copies and go through this process for each goal. You can then prioritize which goal should be worked on first. Welcome to planning and achieving your goals faster and easier than before!

STEP ONE:
IDENTIFYING THE GOAL AND ITS IMPORTANCE

The goal I want to achieve is:

_____

_____

_____

The reason I want to achieve this goal is:

_____

_____

_____

My life would change in the following manner if I achieved my goal:

_____

_____

_____

I would be happier if I achieved my goal because:

_____

_____

_____

The answers to the above questions have made me realize that I am truly willing to commit the time, energy, emotions, and resources necessary to achieve my goal: _____ Yes _____ No

STEP TWO: OUTLINING THE STEPS

I am now committed to my goal and ready to determine what I have to do in order to achieve my goal. There are several steps I must take to make my goal a reality. The five to ten most important things I have to do to achieve my goal are (please list the steps below numbered in order of importance):

_____

_____

_____

_____

_____

_____

_____

_____

_____

_____

_____

_____

_____

_____

_____

_____

_____

STEP THREE: THE TIMELINE

I am committed to achieve my goal no later than _____, 20__.

In will complete the steps I listed on the previous page by the times indicated below (re-list your steps from the prior page and indicate when each can be realistically completed):

STEP DESCRIPTION   **TIME COMPLETED**

_____

_____

_____

_____

_____

_____

_____

_____

_____

_____

_____

_____

_____

_____

_____

_____

_____

_____

STEP FOUR: RESOURCE INVENTORY

In order to achieve my goal and the interim steps toward it, I will need to have a variety of resources. I know I will need to commit time, energy, and emotion to the goal. There may be other resources I need such as money, technical help from someone other than myself or support from those around me. In this section, I am going to identify the resources I need, where they will come from, and, if I don't currently have the resource, how I will get it. This will give me a blueprint for marshalling the resources I need to achieve my goal.

Resource No 1: Time

In order to achieve my goal, I need _____ hours per day/week/month (circle one). I currently have that time available. _____Yes _____No. If I do not have that time currently available, I am going to create it by:

_____

Resource No 2: Energy

In order to achieve my goal, I need energy to work on the goal. I currently have that energy available. _____Yes _____No. If I do not have that energy currently available, I am going to create it by:

_____

Resource No 3: Emotion

In order to achieve my goal, I need emotion and motivation to work on the goal. I currently have that emotion and motivation available. _____

Yes _____No. If I do not have that emotion and motivation currently available, I am going to create it by:

_____

Resource No 4: Money

In order to achieve my goal, I need money in the amount of $_____ as working capital and $_____ in savings so that I can work on my goal free of monetary fear. I currently have that money available. _____Yes

_____No. If I do not have that money available, I need $_____ more. Below, I have listed how I am going to fund my goal, where I am going to find the money, and what steps I have to take to put the money at my disposal:

_____
_____
_____
_____
_____
_____
_____
_____

Coaching is for Everyone

If you need resources other than the four listed above, I have provided space on the next few pages to define the specific resource and how you will get it.

Resource No 5: _____

In order to achieve my goal, I need _____. I currently have this resource available. _____Yes _____No. If I do not have it available, I can get it or create it. Below, I have listed how I am going to create the resource, where I am going to find the resource, and what steps I have to take to put the resource at my disposal:

Resource No 6: _____

In order to achieve my goal, I need _____. I currently have this resource available. _____Yes _____No. If I do not have it available, I can get it or create it. Below, I have listed how I am going to create the resource, where I am going to find the resource, and what steps I have to take to put the resource at my disposal:

Resource No 7: _____

In order to achieve my goal, I need _____. I currently have this resource available. _____Yes _____No. If I do not have it available, I can get it or create it. Below, I have listed how I am going to create the resource, where I am going to find the resource, and what steps I have to take to put the resource at my disposal:

THE FINAL STEP: MEASURING PROGRESS

I want to be sure that, once I start working on my plan, I know that I am moving closer to achieving my goal. In order to do that, I would like to be able to measure my progress along the way. Below I have listed the times when I will stop and measure my progress. I have also listed what must have occurred by that time in order for me to know that I am moving closer to achieving my goal. I will use these measurements to correct my course, inspire me, and keep me moving forward until my goal is achieved.

Date of Measurement: _____, 20____

Description of Progress That Will Have Occurred:

_____

_____

_____

Date of Measurement: _____, 20____

Description of Progress That Will Have Occurred:

_____

_____

_____

Date of Measurement: _____, 20____

Description of Progress That Will Have Occurred:

_____

_____

_____

Coaching is for Everyone

Date of Measurement: _____, 20_____

Description of Progress That Will Have Occurred:

_____

_____

_____

Date of Measurement: _____, 20_____

Description of Progress That Will Have Occurred:

_____

_____

_____

CONGRATULATIONS! YOU HAVE FINISHED CREATING A
GREAT PLAN TO ACHIEVE YOUR GOAL. START NOW AND
USE YOUR PLAN TO MAKE YOUR GOAL AND YOUR DREAM A REALITY.

APPENDIX II

THE MONEY ASSESSMENT

1. My biggest money problem is:

   _____

   _____

2. I fear this problem because:

   _____

   _____

3. My other attitudes toward this problem are:

   _____

   _____

4. I currently handle this money problem by:

   _____

   _____

5. My current attitudes and way of handling this problem are:

   a. solving the problem.   ____yes ____no

   b. creating peace of mind for me.   ____yes ____no

   c. allowing the problem to continue ____yes ____no

   d. draining my energy   ____yes ____no

6. If I eliminated my money problem, I would feel and act differently in the following ways:

_____

_____

7. If I changed my attitude towards my money problem, I would feel and act differently in the following ways:

_____

_____

8. In order to eliminate my money problem, I am committed to taking the following actions now:

_____

_____

9. In order to change my attitude toward my money problem, I am committed to thinking about the problem differently. My new attitude towards this problem is:

_____

_____

10. I want to be fully and completely in control of my attitude toward and dealings with my money. The three things I am committed to doing to start achieving that goal are:

_____

_____

Now that you have done away with your money related issues, how about being free from a cluttered life? All you need is some springtime cleaning and sprucing up your life. And the reward is an outstanding positive personality, a life full of cheerful vitality and relationships that last a lifetime!

APPENDIX III

ELIMINATING LEFTOVERS ONCE AND FOR ALL

1. The three things from my past or present that negatively occupy my thoughts are:

_____

_____

_____

2. I recognize that I tell myself stories based on the things I have listed above. The stories I tell myself about each thought are:

_____

_____

_____

_____

_____

3. If I stopped thinking about the things I listed above and invested that time, energy, and emotion elsewhere, I would add the following positive actions to my life:

_____

_____

_____

_____

_____

4. I'm ready to give up getting energy from and giving energy to these negatives in my life because:

_____

_____

_____

_____

5. In order to take control of this area, I will take action to either be finished with the negative or change my attitude so that the negative does not impact me, or both. For each leftover I listed in number one, here are the actions I am going to take, or attitudes I am going to change, in order to be fully and finally done with each leftover:

_____

_____

_____

_____

_____

6. If I eliminated my money problem, I would feel and act differently in the following ways:

_____

_____

_____

_____

_____

_____

_____

_____

_____

APPENDIX IV

THE TRUTH AND NOTHING BUT THE TRUTH ASSESSMENT

This is a voyage of discovery that is always a little difficult. Please be brutally honest about the answers to these questions, even if it is uncomfortable and difficult.

1. In the last week, I have told the following "little white lies:"

_____

_____

2. In the last week, I have omitted to tell the truth when:

_____

_____

3. In the last week, I have exaggerated the truth when:

_____

_____

4. In the last week, I have not told the whole truth when:

_____

_____

5. As I look at the answers to these questions, I notice that I do not tell the truth when I am afraid of:

_____

_____

Coaching is for Everyone

6. When I look at the answers to questions 1-4, I realize that I do not tell the truth when I want to appear as though I:

_____

_____

7. If I had told the truth in the above situations, the worst things that would have happened are:

_____

_____

8. If I had told the truth in the above situations, what positives would have resulted for me:

_____

_____

9. If I had told the truth in the above situations, how would I have felt different about myself:

_____

_____

10. If I had told the truth in the above situations, what fears would I have left behind:

_____

_____

_____

11. If I commit to telling the whole truth, my rewards would include:

_____

_____

_____

_____

_____

BONUS

$400 Worth of Additional Value Added,
Fresh Content, Tools and Tips!

Special gifts for *Coaching is For Everyone* readers!

Spiritual Laws of a Life Coach, (mp3) - experience Terri's energy and passion as she shares some coaching secrets and her spiritual formula for coaching, living AND creating an EXTRAordinary life!

The 5 Minute Coach - newsletter filled with Terri's tips and tools delivered by email to you every Monday

Coaching For An Extraodinary Life - complete e-book by Terri filled with additional coaching skills

Living an Extraordinary Life - Combined wisdom of high-performing personal and business coaches in e-book format

Magnetizing: The Guidebook to Achieving Financial, Emotional and Spiritual Abundance - Terri's complete e-book teaching you how to get what you want without struggle or effort

Random Musings of a Master Coach - 90 page PDF e-book of some of Terri's most requested, most popular articles, 'musings', and "Dear Reader" letters from over the years - articles that received the most feedback or most requests for repeats

How to Turn Your Passion Into Profits in 30 Days - Are you thinking about becoming a full or part time coach? Wondering if the coaching business is for you? Unsure what it takes to start a coaching business? Then this special report will help guide you

Becoming a Coach In Every Day Life - Ten ways you can become more valuable to everyone you encounter

Free Interactive Quiz to see if you have what it takes to be a coach!

Sounds of Coaching - Free subscription to Terri's 5 Minute Coaching Pod cast

Making the Transition to Coaching Full Time - mp3 audio - what you need to know to be successful

The Truth about the Coaching Industry - mp3 format of a fascinating call where Terri Levine tells it all

Ready to get your free gifts?

Go to:

www.CoachingIsForEveryoneBook.com

to grab yours today!